The
NATURAL
HEALTH
CAT CARE
MANUAL

The NATURAL HEALTH CAT CARE MANUAL

AN INNOVATIVE GUIDE TO KEEPING YOUR CAT IN THE BEST OF HEALTH, NATURALLY

DON HARPER

CHARTWELL
BOOKS INC.

A QUINTET BOOK

Published by Chartwell Books
A Division of Book Sales, Inc.
110 Enterprise Avenue
Secaucus, New Jersey 07094

This edition produced for sale in the U.S.A., its
territories and dependencies only.

ISBN 1–55521–970–5

This book was designed and produced by
Quintet Publishing Limited
6 Blundell Street
London N7 9BH

Creative Director: Richard Dewing
Designer: Wayne Blades
Project Editor: Stefanie Foster
Editor: Janice Anderson
Photography: Marc Henrie, Bradley Viner
Illustrator: Rowan Clifford

Typeset in Great Britain by
Central Southern Typesetters, Eastbourne
Manufactured in Singapore
by Eray Scan Pte Limited
Printed in Singapore
by Star Standard Industries Pte Limited

*This book is in no way intended as a substitute for
veterinary advice. If you suspect that your cat is ill,
always seek qualified veterinary assistance without
delay and follow the instructions given for its subsequent care implicitly. Neither author nor publishers
can accept any liability whatsoever for the use of
remedies included in this book.*

CONTENTS

INTRODUCTION

Interest in natural health care for pets, including cats, has increased significantly during recent years. This mirrors our own awareness that the way in which we live, including what we eat, is likely to exert a direct influence on our state of health.

How to keep a cat healthy is therefore a major theme of this book, in terms of both its diet and its lifestyle. The information given here about illness and its treatments is not intended as a guide to supplanting veterinary involvement in the care of your cat. The diagnosis of feline ailments and their treatment is strictly the responsibility of a qualified veterinarian. Instead, this book seeks to explain some of the trends which are emerging in veterinary care, using techniques that are sometimes referred to as "alternative medicine".

If you prefer this approach to be used whenever practical, then you should register your cat with a veterinarian who uses these methods. Homoeopathic associations help maintain lists of veterinarians who are sympathetic to using these forms of treatment. Another option is simply to telephone local veterinary practices in your area and ask if they would be willing to treat your cat with homoeopathic remedies, basing your choice on their responses.

ALTERNATIVE MEDICINE FOR CATS

There are numerous situations in the medical treatment of animals where alternative medical techniques used on people can be of value.

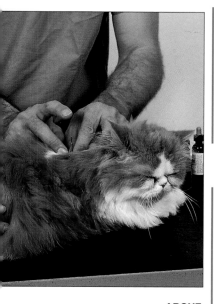

The use of the term "alternative medicine" is rather misleading for these different types of treatment, if only because they are not mutually exclusive. This is why the description "complementary medicine" is more accurate. A combination of treatments may even be considered preferable in some cases, as in the use of acupuncture and herbalism, rather than using one form of therapy on its own.

COMPLEMENTARY MEDICINES

Acupuncture has been used successfully in animals to curb pain and in situations where anaesthesia could be hazardous. Like other alternative techniques, it is not new, having originated in China over 5000 years ago.

Acupuncturists consider that any interference with the body's natural energy can cause health problems. Their technique entails unlocking the blockage, following a thorough examination, by means of very fine needles inserted at specific points in the body. While in veterinary medicine acupuncture is used primarily for purposes of treatment, in human medicine it is also considered to have a prophylactic value in preventing illness.

Acupuncture may be combined with herbal treatment. The dried leaves of the herb mugwort *(Artemisia vulgaris)* are traditionally burnt on the needle's shaft, in a process called moxibustion, to heat the needle and add to its potency.

ACUPUNCTURE

ABOVE
A cat being treated by means of acupuncture. This is becoming increasingly used in the veterinary sphere. Acupuncture relates to the body's energy field, specifically the so-called poles in the body. The yang is positive, whereas the yin is negative, an imbalance resulting in illness.

BELOW
Increasing numbers of veterinarians offer osteopathy, homoeopathy and chiropractic for cats. These treatments can be applied from kitten-hood onwards.

Acupuncture is, of course, a very skilled technique, requiring expert knowledge and not something that the average cat-owner could contemplate practising on their pet. The same is true of chiropractic, which is a manipulative technique, well-established in the field of human medicine to combat spinal injuries or joint disorders. It can be beneficial to cats, particularly after injury, though it is usually used in conjunction with more conventional diagnostic techniques such as X-rays.

CHIROPRACTIC

Whereas chiropractors tend to concentrate on the nervous system in their work, osteopathy is more concerned with massage to achieve a similar effect. Again, this can have applications in the veterinary field, but is not widely used with cats. The differences between chiropractic and osteopathy are dwindling as practitioners absorb more of each other's techniques.

OSTEOPATHY

HOMOEOPATHY

ABOVE
Animals sometimes appear to have instincts about the benefits of plants when they are sick. Cats troubled by fur balls often resort to eating grass.

The biggest impact complementary medicine has made on veterinary care has been on medication itself. Some confusion does exist, particularly between homoeopathy and herbalism, which represent two quite different approaches to dealing with illness. Both are ancient forms of treatment, developed well before the present era of antibiotics and similar synthesized compounds.

Homoeopathy dates back to the days of the ancient Greeks. Its name reflects this link, being derived from *homoios*, a Greek word meaning "like". The rationale behind homoeopathy is that symptoms displayed as the result of an illness are, in reality, the attempts of the body to overcome the disease process. In contrast, conventional veterinary thinking proposes that symptoms are the direct result of the disease rather than the body's reaction to it.

HERBALISM

Herbalism may appear to have more in common with current therapy, especially since a number of the drugs used in veterinary practice today were originally derived from plants. But herbalists consider disease to be the result of imbalances within the body. Although a cat may be suffering from a particular illness, the cause may be addressed by different means, rather than a standard therapeutic approach. Each case is individual and is treated accordingly.

Herbal treatments do not rely on seeking out an active ingredient from a plant, but value the entire plant, which contains' not only the active medical ingredient but also vitamins and trace elements which are believed to aid recovery from illness.

In contrast to conventional therapeutic treatments, those used by herbalists are unlikely to result in allergic reactions. They can be very valuable in combating minor ailments which may be linked to dietary deficiencies. Not suprisingly, herbs are widely used by cat owners as food supplements. They may even be incorporated into some canned diets.

DISTINGUISHING MEDICINES AND SUPPLEMENTS

It is important to be able to distinguish among the various kinds of herbal products on offer. Only those sold as medicines are licensed and tested for efficiency, as well as for purity of ingredients and safety. They may be in tablet form, and even coated with sugar, to disguise the ingredients. Herbal supplements, in contrast, are not subject to such controls, and are typically used alongside the cat's regular diet.

There are other aspects to complementary medicine than just the treatment of disease. For behavioural problems, in particular, practitioners of complementary medicine are turning to Bach Flower Remedies. Named after Dr Edward Bach, who pioneered their use, these are made from special flowers, which are submerged in pure water and warmed by the beneficial rays of sunlight. It is thought that such remedies may have a soothing effect, and so they can be used after shock or trauma in the field of feline medicine, as well as in cases of aggression.

BACH FLOWER REMEDIES

USING COMPLEMENTARY REMEDIES

Obviously, if your cat is ill, you should consult your veterinarian without delay, so that the problem can be diagnosed and appropriate treatment prescribed. In the case of homoeopathic or herbal medicines, these are likely to look just like other prescribed medicines. They may be supplied in the form of tablets, liquids or even granules.

READ THE DOSAGE NOTES CAREFULLY

Dosage instructions should be followed carefully, to maximize the chances of a successful outcome. It is best to give the medication directly to your cat rather than try to disguise it in food, because cats often have an unerring ability to recognize a tablet and leave it in the food bowl. Many such remedies should be given on their own, without food, a fact which will be noted on the label or accompanying instructions.

HOW TO GIVE A TABLET

Giving a tablet to a cat is not especially difficult, provided that the animal is cooperative. Lift your cat onto a suitable table and, ideally, have someone else standing by to restrain it around the sides of its body. Gently tilt the cat's head upwards and, placing your left hand around the sides of the cat's mouth, hold the upper jaw. Push down on the lower jaw with your right hand, and then slip the tablet as far back on the cat's tongue as possible. The advantages of holding the head up is that the tablet should fall backwards in the mouth. Then close the jaws immediately, keeping the head tilted and tickle the cat on its throat. This will encourage it to swallow the tablet and prevent it from spitting the tablet out. Most cats do not resent this procedure, but if you encounter difficulty or are nervous of handling your cat in this way for fear of being bitten or scratched, you may find that a pill dispenser will be easier. This simply serves to pop the tablet into the cat's mouth.

BELOW
Grasp the cat's head firmly on either side of the jaw (1). Bend the head gently but firmly backward until the lower jaw begins to drop open (2). Push the tablet onto the "V" right at the back of the cat's throat. It may go down more easily if it is lubricated with a bit of butter (3).

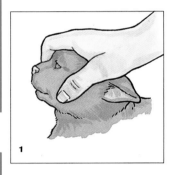

GIVING LIQUID MEDICINES

Liquid medicines are often harder to administer than tablets, because there is no easy way of ensuring that the cat swallows the fluid. Almost inevitably, some will trickle out of the mouth. It may be possible, with a cooperative patient, to open the mouth and pour in a small quantity of fluid from a dropper or spoon, taking care not to choke the cat. Alternatively, you will need to run the fluid in from the side of the mouth using a small plastic syringe, without a needle attached, for the purpose. (Do not use a glass dropper

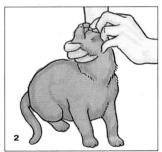

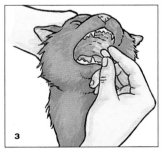

RIGHT
Care is needed to ensure that a cat cannot wriggle free when being dosed with a liquid medicine. A helping hand is to be recommended for this purpose.

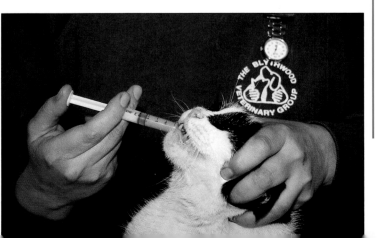

of any kind, as it could break in the cat's mouth, with serious consequences.) The relative gap behind the long canine teeth at the front of the jaw is the best position for giving liquid medicines. The syringe will make the task easier, because there is less risk of the medicine being spilled, but do not push the plunger too fast. Instead, allow the medication to flow out steadily in the mouth, pausing if your cat starts coughing and allowing it to lower its head.

BELOW
The nutritional needs of kittens, such as this pure-bred Chinchilla Longhair, differ from those of adult cats. Special diets or supplements can be used. This should be discussed with your veterinarian.

Since cats drink relatively little, it is almost impossible to dispense any medicine successfully via drinking water, although granules can be mixed in with food, as can most supplements. These tend to be quite palatable; yeast, for example, which is a valuable source of B vitamins, is taken readily by cats, in powdered form, sprinkled over food or simply as a tablet.

SUPPLEMENTS IN FOOD AND DRINK

HOW LONG TO GIVE MEDICATION

Depending on the condition, medication may need to be given over a period which can last up to several weeks or more. You will find the times for specific treatments in the chapter on Health Care. Although incorrect dosing is obviously to be avoided, this is less likely to have serious side-effects than with modern drugs.

STORING MEDICINES AND SUPPLEMENTS

Homoeopathic and herbal remedies should be stored under similar conditions to drugs, in dry containers, preferably out of the light in a medical cabinet. As a general rule, they should remain suitable for use for at least five years when kept in the right conditions.

HOMOEOPATHIC REMEDIES

While a number of treatments can be purchased without a prescription, some homoeopathic medicines must be prescribed, as must homoeopathic alternatives to conventional inoculations against the serious viral diseases that can afflict cats. These products are known as nosodes and oral vaccines, and they can be used to prevent disease, in a prophylactic manner, and therapeutically, if the need arises.

NOSODES AND ORAL VACCINES

The term "nosode" is derived from the Greek word for disease, *nosos*. Such products are obtained from an animal afflicted with the disease for which the inoculation is required. The disease-causing micro-organism may not be present, but this is not considered significant, because it is the products produced by the body in combating the illness that underline the efficiency of the nosode rather than the virus itself. In some cases, typically those which have proved refractory to treatment, autonosodes are prepared. These are based on material obtained from the sick cat itself.

There is a degree of overlap between nosodes and oral vaccines, although the latter are derived specifically from the harmful micro-organism responsible for the disease or from their toxins. In the case of bacteria, an oral vaccine may be made from an emulsion, comprising both bacteria and toxins, or a filtrate that contains just toxins. The appropriate oral vaccine can not only act to guard against a disease but can also have a curative role, giving rise to rapid recovery in cases where there is no long-term problem.

The so-called group of bowel nosodes are more accurately described as oral vaccines, because they are manufactured directly from micro-organisms cultured for this purpose. These are used primarily in chronic cases, where previous sustained treatment has not been successful and several different treatments appear to be indicated.

There are five main bowel nosodes, each of which has specific functions and may be used in conjunction with other appropriate remedies and have far-reaching effects in the body. They may be given daily over a short period of time, and then used again several months later if required.

BOWEL NOSODES

RIGHT
Homoeopathy utilises specially prepared nosodes to give protection against the main killer viral diseases of cats. Young cats, in particular, can benefit from nosodes.

The potency of a homoeopathic remedy is a reference to the strength of the medication being used. This may typically vary from 3c to 200c, with the letter "c" simply serving to indicate a pharmacological code, based on the centesimal scale, whereas "x" refers to a decimal scale. The number in this instance refers to the dilution factor which has been used.

The so-called mother tincture, sometimes indicated simply as "0", is the starting point made from the substance to be used. This is then typically diluted with alcohol, with one drop being added to 99 parts of alcohol in the first instance. This gives a dilution factor of 1:100, written in the shorthand code as 1c. If diluted again, there will then be one unit of mother tincture in 10,000 parts of alcohol, to create a 2c preparation. A 200c description confirms that the solution has been successively diluted through 200 stages. The higher the number preceding the letter, the more dilute is the solution, but the more potent is the remedy.

"POTENCY" EXPLAINED

SUCCUSSION Each dilution is carefully prepared, being shaken on a hard surface for a specific period of time, to ensure thorough mixing. The procedure is called "succussion." While even a 3c solution reflects just one part of mother tincture in 1,000,000, higher dilutions are made, to the point where, it has been suggested, the preparations are so dilute that they contain no active ingredients from the original mother tincture.

Nevertheless, homoeopaths are convinced of their efficacy and point to their success, particularly in the veterinary field, where there is no psychosomatic component identified. Quite simply, a cat does not become ill for a psychological reason and then recover simply on the basis of a placebo effect.

Giving a cat something that is claimed to be medicinal will in no way contribute to its recovery, as sometimes happens with people. In fairness, however, the possibility remains that the cat might have recovered satisfactorily on its own, without any medication being prescribed.

TRITURATION Not all substances used in homoeopathy are soluble in alcohol, and these must be potentiated by a different process. Sulphur and mercury are two widely used elements in this category.

The preparation of medications containing such items is more demanding, but is still achieved by means of successive dilutions, usually carried out at first with milk sugar. Instead of a drop, grains are used, starting with one grain of the element, and 100 grains of milk sugar. These are ground together in a process known as "trituration".

One part of this powder is mixed with a further 100 grains of sugar, still resulting in a solid potency at this stage. After the third dilution, or 3c stage, it is usually possible to carry out successive dilutions with alcohol, in the normal fashion, marking the commencement of liquid potency. The actual stage varies according to the component concerned; in the case of *Silicea*, it may not be reached until the 6c stage.

In the early days of homoeopathy, the preparation of remedies was very laborious and time-consuming. Today, with the advent of highly efficient technology, these dilutions can be made very rapidly and effectively, although some components of the process, such as shaking the preparation after a dilution, may still be carried out manually in some instances.

The primary sources of homoeopathic medicines vary, although plants are the main source. More than 60 per cent of the 2,500 or so homoeopathic treatments used today are of plant origin, drawn from around the world. As more of the world's plants are studied for their healing powers, these figures are likely to increase. At present, barely 25,000 of the 500,000 plants on the planet have been assessed in these terms.

The scientific name of the plant forms the basis for naming the resulting homoeopathic medicine, enabling it to be identified easily anywhere in the world; common plant names tend to be localized in their usage, and so would be less suitable. The potentiated remedy produced from deadly nightshade is therefore known as *Belladonna*. While this is a well-recognized pharmacologically active plant, which can cause fatal poisoning if consumed in its natural state, not all homoeopathic plant sources are so evident. Club moss spores, for instance, must first be triturated before they become active, assisting with the treatment of both gastric and renal disorders, under the name of *Lycopodium clavatum*.

WHERE HOMOEOPATHIC MEDICINES COME FROM

The stage at which the plant must be gathered can be critical. In the case of *Belladonna*, this should occur after flowering, with the entire plant being used. In other remedies, just part of the plant, shrub or tree may be required. *Cinchona officinalis*, also known as Peruvian bark, was the source of the first anti-malarial compound, quinine. Its bark is also used in other homoeopathic remedies, typically prescribed after diarrhoea, for example.

The roots of water hemlock (*Cicuta virosa*), gathered at the time of flowering, are used for the treatment of ailments affecting the central nervous system. In contrast, the powdered seeds of Indian Cockle (*Cocculus*) can fulfil a similar role, being used primarily for cats suffering from travel sickness.

Minerals, including precious metals such as gold, silver and platinum, are also used in homoeopathic preparations. Platinum, under the name Platina, is favoured for dealing with disorders of the female genital system, such as cystic ovaries. In the case of cats, it is often used with breeds of

GATHERING HOMOEOPATHIC PLANTS

eastern ancestry, such as the Siamese and Burmese.

Potencies of salts are usually prepared slightly differently from other remedies. Ammonium carbonicum is made initially by dissolving ammonium carbonate in distilled water, which is then diluted. The salt Antimonium crudum, which is antimony sulphide, requires trituration initially to make it soluble.

HOMOEOPATHIC REMEDIES FROM ANIMALS

A very diverse range of animal products feature in homoeopathic remedies. These include bee venom, formic acid from ants, the contents of the ink sac of cuttlefish, eel serum and the shell of oysters, with the method of preparation depending on the substance concerned.

A WARNING ON DOSAGE

CLEARLY, A NUMBER OF THE PRODUCTS USED FOR HOMOEOPATHIC TREATMENT WOULD BE DEADLY IF NOT CORRECTLY PREPARED. THIS IS NOT AN AREA FOR EXPERIMENTATION INVOLVING YOUR CAT, AND ONLY CORRECTLY POTENTIZED FORMULATIONS, DESCRIBED IN THIS BOOK AND OBTAINED FROM VETERINARIANS, SHOULD BE USED FOR TREATMENT PURPOSES. THE CONCEPT THAT A LITTLE MAY BE OF SOME BENEFIT, SO A MORE CONCENTRATED SOLUTION WILL BE OF GREATER VALUE, IS NEVER MORE MISPLACED THAN IN THE FIELD OF HOMOEOPATHY.

THE ORIGINS OF MODERN HOMOEOPATHY

Modern homoeopathy was pioneered by a German doctor, Samuel Hahnemann, in the late 18th century, although its origins date back as far as the 10th century BC. Hahnemann first proposed the *Similia* law, and introduced the term homoeopathy in 1796, continuing to develop his ideas up to his death in 1843. He saw the administration of a diluted form of a substance similar to that causing the disease process as providing a means for the body to respond in such a way that it reacted positively not only to the medication, but also to the disease, overcoming it as a consequence. The homoeopathic remedy served as a catalyst, to trigger the body's defence mechanism.

In this respect, there are some parallels between homoeopathy and immunization, especially where so-called live yet potentiated vaccines are used. Administering a controlled dose of a virus, for example, back to a cat, causes the animal's body to react to it, activating its immune system to protect it. The use of serum for treatment purposes is another example, when protection is achieved by exposure to the pathogenic micro-organism.

ABOVE
A woodcut of Samuel Hahnemann, who is considered to be the founding father of modern homoeopathy. His methods, dating from the late 1700s, are still in use today.

The means by which the efficacy of potential remedies is tested was pioneered by Hahnemann. He read how Peruvian bark could reduce the temperature peaks associated with malarial fever, but disagreed with its suggested effects. By dosing himself with the bark extract, known as "china", Hahnemann noted in 1791 that it then produced similar symptoms to malaria. He formed the opinion that its efficacy for treatment purposes relied upon the fact that it produced similar symptoms to malaria in a healthy person. This was the trigger which began Hahnemann's interest in what he subsequently named homoeopathy.

Since then, a wide variety of substances has been taken by volunteers, using Hahnemann's directions, to test their effects on the body. The resulting symptoms are noted, making it possible to formulate the potential applications of these substances for therapeutic purposes. The remedies themselves are then known as "provings", with those who took the substance initially being known as "provers". Homoeopathic remedies are therefore not dependent on animal testing, but can certainly be of value to all animals (even to fish).

From the outset, Hahnemann set out guidelines for provers, being aware of the need to safeguard their health while obtaining meaningful results. Such people needed to be healthy and able to note and report their findings accurately. He recommended that their diet should be kept simple and free from herbs and vegetables, which might themselves exert an effect.

Provings today are conducted on rather similar lines, but significantly, placebos, which mimic the appearance of the substance under test but are physiologically and pharmacologically inert, now play a role. This reduces the likelihood of bias resulting from the fact that the prover knows that he is taking a drug. Only those running the proving know which provers are receiving the placebos; this serves to eliminate any possible psychosomatic component in the results.

"PROVING" HOMOEOPATHIC REMEDIES

While provings have been very significant in the development of homoeopathy, study of toxicology has also been shown to be of value. In Hahnemann's time, mercury was the favoured therapy for syphilis, but overdosing would result in serious side-effects. Ulceration of the mouth and the intestinal lining, as well as vomiting and diarrhoea, were all well-recognized complications.

HOMOEOPATHY AND TOXICOLOGY

By using homoeopathic mercurial preparations, Hahnemann was able to treat similar complaints successfully. Today in veterinary practice, a range of mercurius formulations are in use for various ailments, including otitis media, inflammation of the middle ear, where pus is present. A single, high potency dose is given in this instance.

Another early application of toxicology in the development of homoeopathic remedies occurred in 1828. One of Hahnemann's supporters, Constantine Herring, was searching for plants in the Upper Amazon region in South America, where he learnt from the natives about a deadly venomous snake, known locally as the surukuku, now better known to science as the Bushmaster (*Lachesis muta*).

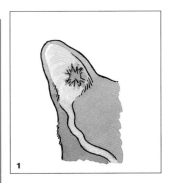

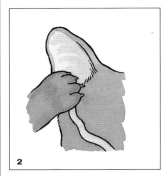

BELOW
The venom of the deadly Bushmaster snake from South America is now used in homoeopathic treatments for various conditions. Not all homoeopathic remedies originate from plants.

Herring offered a reward for a live specimen but was abandoned by the natives when they realized that he intended to handle the one obtained for him in order to collect its venom. Having stunned it with a blow to the head, Herring managed to milk out the venom from the glands on to milk sugar. He then began to prepare a low potency preparation from it, only to be overcome by delirium, before sleep intervened. These effects of working at close quarters with this venom were then recorded by Herring after his recovery, and served to provide the initial proving by *Lachesis*.

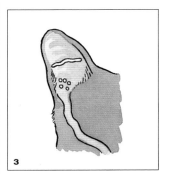

Subsequent provings were carried out at a 30c potency, because of the obvious dangers. A variety of effects, including dizziness, a tight-chested feeling and bruising were noted. Today, *Lachesis* can be used for the homoeopathic treatment of various feline conditions, ranging from throat ailments to snake bites.

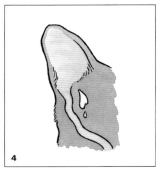

A trigger factor such as ear mites causes an irritation of the ear (**1**), which causes the cat to scratch the ear (**2**), which then causes further trauma and inflammation (**3**), allowing ideal conditions for secondary bacterial or fungal infection to grow (**4**). This may eventually lead to chronic inflammation and thickening of the lining of the ear canal (**5**).

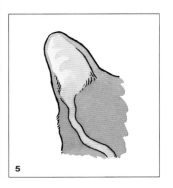

ABOVE
Feline dysautonomia causes a
paralysis of the autonomic
nervous system, that
subconsciously controls certain
body functions. This cat shows
the distinctive dilated pupils,
unresponsive to light, that is
typical in many cases.

Over the 200 years since Hahnemann began his work records based both on provings and toxicology have been carefully maintained. This has enabled prescribing manuals, referred to as *Materia Medica*, to be built up. Within such works are listed substances with their observed effects, and their resulting homoeopathic potential for the treatment of various conditions.

There is also a second system of recording homoeopathic data, based on symptoms rather than on substances. These are described as repertoires, and they list the symptoms first, as the reference point, followed by possible appropriate treatments. Yet each case still needs to be judged on an individual basis, particularly in the case of animals such as cats, which are unable to describe their symptoms.

New diseases such as Feline Dysautonomia, which affects the nervous system and was known initially as the Key–Gaskell Syndrome, arise and present new challenges for veterinary homoeopathy. The actual cause of this condition has still to be elucidated. Even so, several homoeopathic remedies have assisted cats suffering from the illness.

THE HOMOEOPATHIC RECORD

HERBALISM AND ITS APPLICATIONS

In the broadest sense, herbs are plants that are of value to people and animals, for a wide variety of purposes. Three different herb types have long been recognized as foods: sweet herbs, now referred to as culinary herbs, such as sage; salad herbs, which have long been valued for the table; and pot herbs such as onions, which have become better known as vegetables. Although there are obvious botanical differences between them, fungi may also be considered as herbal plants.

Interest in herbs as a basis for treatment dates back many thousands of years. Initially, plants with a hallucinatory effect may have focused attention on the treatment possibilities of herbs. The Chinese had started practising herbal medicine by 2700 BC and the tradition spread from there, being developed in Europe by the Greeks and Romans.

BELOW
Onion (*Allium cepa*) is a valuable source of vitamins, as well as being helpful in dealing with respiratory infections, and gastro-enteritis.

BELOW
Saga (*Salvia officinalis*). Its scientific name *Salvia* is derived from the Latin word *salvere*, meaning "in good health". It has various properties, including antiseptic action.

HERBALISM TODAY

There have been significant changes over the centuries, with few of today's herbalists using the potentially poisonous plants which used to be favoured in medieval times. Indeed, one of the characteristics of herbalism today is that the remedies are safe, and are not associated with adverse side-effects.

Herbs are often used alone for treatment purposes, being described as *simples* under these circumstances. Occasionally, several different herbs may be used together. With herbs, as with homoeopathy or, indeed, conventional medicine, it is vital first to obtain an accurate diagnosis of an animal's illness from a veterinarian. The appropriate herbal treatment can then be commenced.

CHOOSING THE CORRECT TREATMENT

THERE ARE SOME CONTRA-INDICATIONS, EVEN WITH HERBAL MEDICINES. FOR EXAMPLE, IT WOULD BE SENSIBLE NOT TO DOSE A PREGNANT CAT WITH PENNYROYAL (*MENTHA PULEGIUM*), BECAUSE THIS MAY CAUSE IT TO ABORT, WHILE CATS WHICH HAVE A HISTORY OF CALCULI (STONES) IN THE URINARY TRACT SHOULD NOT BE PROVIDED WITH RHUBARB (*RHEUM OFFICINALE*) IF THEY BECOME CONSTIPATED.

MAKING HERBAL TREATMENTS

Herbal treatments are available in a range of forms, which may relate to the way in which the active ingredient has been extracted, as well as the way in which it is going to be used. The different parts of the plant may also contain active ingredients in varying proportions. Extraction methods mean that in most cases making herbal treatments cannot be carried out satisfactorily at home, though there are certain processes which are possible at home, with a variety of herbs. A relatively simple one is infusion, which enables water soluble substances to be extracted from the softer parts of the plants, such as their leaves, stems or flowers.

LEFT
The breed of cat and its medical history should be taken into account when applying herbal remedies. It is important to obtain an accurate diagnosis of the cat's condition before commencing treatment.

When gathering herbs growing wild for infusions it is best to avoid sites that may well be contaminated, such as roadside verges. Here, the level of lead in the vegetation is likely to be higher, because of fumes from passing traffic. Chemicals such as weed killers may have been used, while close to footpaths, dogs are most likely to have soiled the vegetation.

Ideally, you should collect only those herbs that you have grown yourself, because you can then be certain that they will be uncontaminated. The increasing interest both in herbalism and conservation in recent years has made it considerably easier to purchase seed from specialist suppliers. They often advertise in the gardening sections of newspapers, as well as in gardening and wildlife magazines, supplying customers by mail order. With care, most herbs can be grown quite easily from seed and should guarantee a constant source of supply.

LEFT
While cats may not be keen to eat herbs, the production of herbal tablets makes it easier for them to derive benefit from such plants.

MAKING INFUSIONS

To make an infusion, you will need to gather 30 g (1 oz) of plant material, which should first be washed under running water and shaken dry. It must then be chopped up finely, and placed in a suitable lidded container. This can be made of glass, stone or porcelain, but it is important that the lid is tight-fitting, because otherwise volatile substances released during the infusion process will be lost into the surrounding atmosphere.

The plant material should then be covered with 500 ml (20 fl oz) of boiling water, and the lid put in place. It should be left to stand for about 15 minutes, before the liquid is strained off into a separate container and allowed to cool. This can be given to the cat to drink, although it is generally better to pour the infusion over the cat's food, allowing it to be absorbed, since cats will not normally drink a large volume of liquid on its own.

ABOVE
Aside from tablets, it is also possible to administer the benefits of herbs in the form of an infusion, which can then be poured over the cat's food.

DECOCTION

Drier parts of a plant, such as the roots, as well as seeds and bark, need a different treatment, in order to release water-soluble components. This process is known as "decoction". The first step is to soak 30 g (1 oz) of chopped ingredients in 500 ml (20 fl oz) of cold water for 10 minutes or so.

A small glass saucepan with a lid is ideal for this purpose, because the water should next be heated to boiling point, and the contents then allowed to simmer for about 15 minutes. The pan should be left to cool over a further 10-minute period, before the water is drained off. This can then be used in much the same way as an infusion would be.

HERBAL POULTICES

Some herbs can be of benefit when applied directly to the body in the form of a poultice. There are various ways of preparing a poultice. If fresh herbs are used they should be crushed, using a mortar and pestle. They can then be mixed with a little hot water to form a paste that can be used in a poultice.

Alternatively, a poultice can be made up from dried plant matter, softening the herbs in bran, flour or a similar agent which acts as a suspending material. It can be difficult to apply poultices to cats, because of their lithe build and athletic nature, but it can be done with careful bandaging. A thin muslin cloth can be used to maintain a relatively liquid poultice, applied directly to the affected part.

ABOVE
The warmth of a poultice will assist in the healing process. It can be especially valuable in combating abscesses in cats.

HERBS AND
PARASITES

Aside from being of value in illnesses, some herbs are also of particular value in combating parasitic problems. Again, however, the need to rely on veterinary advice before giving any remedy is illustrated by the case of the male fern (*Dryopteris felix-mas*). This has long been known as a means of combating tapeworm infestations, to which cats as hunters are especially susceptible.

This particular fern is widely distributed in temperate parts of the world, and various parts, including the base of the fronds and the dried rhizome, are pharmacologically active, killing tapeworms present in the gut. If used at too high a dose, however, it can cause blindness and even death.

External parasites can also be overcome by herbal means, although, again, caution is essential. Tincture of larkspur (*Delphinium consolida*), made using fresh seeds, will kill lice and similar parasites. Yet cats lick their coats, and could well ingest an unfamiliar substance applied to their fur. Tincture of larkspur, if consumed acts as a strong purgative and can prove poisonous, so it is advisable to use a safer remedy. Herbal treatments which have been produced for people may not always be suitable for cats.

The cat's metabolism also differs somewhat from our own, with the result that remedies of value to us may be lethal if given to cats. The best-known example is acetylsalicylic acid or aspirin. Cats are less able than most mammals to detoxify drugs, breaking them down to safe, simple substances which can be excreted from the body. They simply lack the necessary enzymes for this purpose.

The herbs which may be used safely and effectively with cats are explained in Health Care.

BELOW
Care needs to be taken over remedies applied to the cat's coat, to combat fleas, for example, as they lick their fur frequently, and are likely to ingest any medication present here.

BELOW
Grinding up herbs is traditionally accomplished using a mortar and pestle, as shown here. The resulting powder can then be sprinkled over food.

A NATURAL LIFESTYLE FOR YOUR CAT

When choosing a pet, most people prefer to start with a young kitten rather than an adult cat, in spite of the fact that older cats prove quite adaptable and soon settle well in a new home. They are also likely to be less of a problem initially, in that they will almost certainly be house-trained and may already have been neutered.

... no

PEDIGREE OR MOGGIE?

Aside from the age of the cat, you will also need to decide whether you want a pedigre or a non-pedigree cat. There are approximately fifty basic breeds of cat, available in a wide range of colours and markings. The different breeds show variations in temperament, which need to be taken into account. Orientals, for example, tend to be more lively and demonstrative by nature than the more placid Persian Longhairs. Pedigree cats suffer far less from congenital health problems than many breeds of dog, and this is not generally an area for concern when seeking a kitten. One problem that can arise is extra toes, especially on the front paws, but these do not handicap a cat.

Coat length must also be considered, as short-haired cats need less grooming than their long-haired counterparts. Without regular grooming, not only will the cat's coat become tangled, making combing and brushing a painful experience for your pet, but the likelihood of fur balls forming in the cat's stomach is also greatly increased. Long-haired cats should be groomed every day.

The gender of the cat will be of less significance, unless you are planning to breed cats, in which case a female kitten should be chosen. You can then take her to a stud in due course for a carefully planned mating, thus avoiding adding to the large number of unwanted cats and kittens discarded by thoughtless owners every year.

Many of these find their way into the care of rescue organizations. If you are wanting a moggie rather than a pedigree cat, offering a home to one of these cats is a good way of helping the work of the rescue organizations. Leaving a donation will help to ensure that it can continue, assisting other cats in the future.

BELOW
Longhaired cats need more grooming than their short-haired counterparts, otherwise not only will their coat become matted, but they are also likely to swallow loose hairs as they groom themselves. These will accumulate as a mat in the stomach, resulting in a fur ball.

BELOW
Ragdoll cats are reputedly insensitive to pain, but there is no truth in this story. Their name comes from their habit of relaxing when picked up, so their body becomes limp, like that of a ragdoll.

In general, cats seldom eat vegetation, but they will chew catnip leaves, as well as sniffing repeatedly and pawing at the plant. They may then react by sitting quietly for up to 15 minutes or so, appearing unresponsive to other stimuli nearby, or roll around on the ground, and then shake their heads. Exposure to catnip seems to induce a feeling of contentment in susceptible individuals, but the effects are transitory, since it will be at least an hour before the cat is attracted back to the spot.

Aside from the possible hallucinogenic cause, catnip may mimic chemical constituents of the urine of male cats, which attract the female. This seems a less than plausible explanation, since female cats, whether or not they a ready to mate, and males appear to respond equally to the effects of catnip.

Catnip has been used on occasions as a sedative for cats which are difficult to handle, but the benefits are very transitory, and it is not recommended for this purpose. The effects induced by catnip appear to be relatively unique, although the dried root of garden heliotrope, also known as valerian (*Valeriana officinalis*), may evoke a similar but less pronounced response.

ABOVE
If your cat lives indoors permanently, you can still offer the benefits of fresh grass. Kits for this purpose, which you can grow on the windowsill, can be purchased from many pet shops.

FEEDING

E ven if you intend to alter the diet of your kitten at a later date, you should stick closely to the food and feeding routine to which it has been used, and introduce changes gradually only after a week or so. This will help to minimize the risk of digestive disturbances during the early days.

It is possible, however, to give a "new" cat a probiotic, which could be beneficial after the stress of the journey and being faced with a new environment. A probiotic will serve to stabilize the bacteria in the gut, making it difficult for other, potentially harmful

BELOW
Always encourage kittens to sample a range of foods early in life. This should help to avoid them developing fussy appetites as they grow older.

microbes to gain access, so minimizing the likelihood of any digestive disorder. A range of probiotics is now available, which can be administered simply in the cat's food, without impairing its appetite.

There are other circumstances in which probiotics can be of value, most notably if your pet falls ill and is prescribed a course of antibiotics. These drugs generally kill not only harmful bacteria but also depress the beneficial bacteria in the body, which not only help to protect against further infection, but may produce substances such as vitamin K (a key ingredient in the blood clotting system), which the body requires in order to function effectively.

As a result, although the antibiotics may have overcome the infection, they will also have created a vacuum in the body's defences, leaving the cat potentially vulnerable to further infections. A probiotic given after the antibiotics are completed will be of value, although there is no use giving them with the antibiotics, because their efficacy will be reduced.

RIGHT
Kittens will soon settle in new surroundings, but keep a watch on them to see they do not end up in any trouble when they are first let outdoors. It is important that they get used to the outside environment as soon as possible.

Should you have to hand-rear young kittens, the addition of a probiotic product to their food, on a regular basis, can be of great benefit. While kittens obtain some immunity from their mother's milk in the early days of life, they also require exposure to beneficial bacteria, which can colonize their intestinal tract. Otherwise, they will be exceedingly vulnerable to infection. Contact with their mother and their immediate environment normally is enough to provide this protection, but kittens reared in an artificial environment do not have the same opportunities to acquire it.

THE CAT'S SPECIAL FOOD NEEDS

In order to appreciate the cat's nutritional requirements, it is necessary to look back to their wild ancestor, the African wild cat (*Felis silvestris lybica*), and its diet. These small cats are keen hunters, feeding mainly on small rodents and birds. They eat the whole animal in most cases, including the fur or feathers, which provide roughage.

ABOVE AND LEFT
The natural hunting behaviour of cats can still be seen in domestic moggies. Small rodents and birds form their usual quarry, but more enterprising individuals may take fish from garden ponds.

IMPORTANCE OF ANIMAL PROTEIN

Unlike dogs, which are more omnivorous in their feeding habits, cats cannot be kept satisfactorily on a vegetarian diet. They need a high-protein diet, which must, at least in part, be of animal origin. Cats are sometimes described as being obligate carnivores, as they require meat as a source of protein.

There are many different types of protein, which can be of either animal or plant origin. Proteins are composed of individual amino acid residues, which are linked together in the form of chains. There are 20 amino acids, of which approximately half are described as being "essential". These must be present in the cat's diet if specific deficiencies are not to arise. Proteins that have the highest biological value, containing these essential amino acids, are invariably of animal origin.

Cats, unlike dogs and other mammals, also have a specific requirement for an amino acid called taurine in their diet. Other species can manufacture this in their bodies, but cats cannot. Taurine is vital to ensure that the retina, which is the part of the eye where the image is formed, functions effectively. A deficiency results in degeneration of the retina and ultimately will cause blindness. Only protein of animal origin contains sufficient taurine to meet the cat's needs, which is one particular reason they require meat.

ESSENTIAL TAURINE

RIGHT
Cats have a specific requirement for taurine in their diet. This is the reason as to why dog food is unsuitable for them on a regular basis, since it does not contain sufficient levels of this amino acid for cats. Taurine is vital for healthy eyesight.

Animal tissues are made up essentially of proteins and fats. It is not surprising, therefore, that the fat component of their diet is important for cats. Fat serves to improve the palatability of food, and fats are used in the body in various ways, not least for the manufacture of substances called essential fatty acids, which are vital ingredients of new cells.

Most mammals possess the ability to convert linoleic acid, which is the most widely distributed essential fatty acid, into the other two essential fatty acids. But cats do not possess this ability, and so these additional essential fatty acids, which, unlike linoleic acid, do not occur in vegetable oils, must be present in the diet, in order to prevent a deficiency. This again underlies the significance of meat in a cat's diet.

FAT IS IMPORTANT, TOO

VITAL VITAMIN A

Another peculiarity of the cat's metabolism is its inability to manufacture vitamin A from so-called precursors such as β-carotene, which is present in plants. Without this vital vitamin, cats may become more prone to infections, and their eyesight is likely to be affected. A meat-based diet is again recommended, as a natural source of vitamin A for cats.

These three examples of the cat's particular dietary needs confirm that diets for cats need to be carefully formulated. While an imbalance or deficiency over the course of a day or so is unlikely to be harmful, a persistent dietary failing will soon become manifest in your cat's health.

ABOVE
Some cats can be very playful at feeding time, even to the extent of begging to attract their owner's attention, like a dog.

GOOD FOOD IS EASY

It is rarely acknowledged that one of the major reasons why cats have become so popular as pets is the ease with which they can be fed a diet which will keep them healthy. There is no need to feel guilty about using formulated foods, rather than preparing fresh rations every day, although you may well decide to do this on occasions. It will help to provide variation in your cat's diet, and, in specific circumstances, may also assist recovery in the event of illness, by rekindling the cat's appetite.

With home-cooked cat food you will need to provide sources of animal fat and protein. Carbohydrates are not actually essential, though they can be provide in the form of cooked potatoes or rice, for example, mixed in with other foods. Most butchers will provide pet mince that is suitable for cats, and of course, specific items such as chicken, rabbit and liver can all be used as well. Fish is also popular, and cats will also eat eggs and cheese.

BELOW
Try to feed your cat at regular times each day, and be sure to wash the bowl out thoroughly after each meal. Cats can be very fastidious in their feeding habits.

RAW OR COOKED?

Although studies have shown that cats fed on raw meat may display slightly better growth rates, the benefits are outweighed by the disadvantages. Bacterial contamination is a problem, with uncooked poultry being a potent source of *Salmonella* bacteria. Even if these bacteria do not cause illness, they may establish themselves in the cat's digestive tract, with the cat then becoming a potential *Salmonella* carrier, excreting the bacteria intermittently with its faeces. This could represent a hazard to people and to other household pets.

Similarly, cats can be easily infected by the protozoal parasite known as *Toxoplasma gondii*, which gives rise to the disease known as toxoplasmosis. This can represent a particular threat to pregnant women, because these protozoa can cross the placental barrier, into a baby. The danger period is relatively short, since the cat produces the infective oocysts for only about a fortnight after exposure to the parasite and is not contagious thereafter.

There are also dangers in allowing cats to eat raw fish. In some parts of the world, a tapeworm called *Diphyllobothrium latum*, which is present in the body of freshwater fish, is a hazard. When the larval stage in the tapeworm's life cycle is eaten, the adult tapeworm will develop in the cat.

A more generalized problem relates to the high level of thiaminase present in the body tissue of a number of fish, including herring. Thiaminase is an enzyme which serves to deactivate vitamin B1 or thiamin. As a result, over a period of time cats can develop the nervous signs associated with a deficiency of this vitamin. These can be quite alarming, with the cat actually convulsing in severe cases. Cooking such fish overcomes the problem, because the heat denatures the enzyme so that it is no longer harmful to the cat.

RIGHT
Raw meat is not to be recommended for cats, because it can be a source of harmful microbes and parasites, which will be killed by in cooking process.

COOKING THE CAT'S FOOD AT HOME

The way in which food is cooked has a direct bearing on both its nutritional value and its palatability. A cat's food should never be overcooked, as this will lower the vitamin content, with the B vitamins being particularly vulnerable. Cats also prefer warm food, rather than something served straight from the fridge. This is unsurprising, because they will eat live prey immediately after catching and killing it, while the carcass is still warm.

Cooking food also tends to make it softer and improves its palatability, especially for cats which are off-colour. As a general rule, you are more likely to rekindle your pet's appetite with carefully prepared home-cooked food than with a prepared food straight from a can or packet.

There are distinct health risks in pandering too far to a healthy cat's feeding preferences, when it comes to fresh foods. Adequate variety is essential, and although cats can be fussy when eating, the fact that they avidly consume a particular food should not be taken as a sign that they are receiving a balanced diet and they should accept a varied diet as early as possible.

EASY DOES IT WITH LIVER . . .

Liver, which is very popular with most cats, illustrates this point. Should you allow your cat to feed exclusively on liver on a regular basis, it is very likely to develop symptoms associated with an excess intake of vitamin A. This vitamin is stored in the liver, and must be present in the cat's diet. But if its intake is excessive, the cat could display signs of a stiff neck, with accompanying pain. This may also afflict the legs, resulting in lameness. The cause of the problem is the development of abnormal bony swellings, which cripple the cat. There is no cure – prevention depends upon offering a balanced diet, paying constant attention to the cat's intake.

. . . AND WITH OILY FISH

A similar problem, arising in this case from a vitamin deficiency and a diet of fish, is pansteatitis. Feeding excessive amounts of oily fish such as tuna, which contain high levels of polyunsaturated fat, combined with a shortage of vitamin E, are responsible for this condition. It is sometimes described as yellow fat disease, because of the characteristic change in coloration of the body fat. Cats should therefore not be fed exclusively on such fish on a regular basis, even if they do show a marked preference for it.

Even minced meat on its own is likely to create nutritional deficiencies over a period of time, particularly in the case of kittens. This is because of a serious imbalance in the calcium: phosphorus ratio, which results in a relative deficiency of calcium, the key ingredient of a healthy skeletal system.

Siamese cats are especially prone to this deficiency, with the condition itself sometimes being described as juvenile osteodystrophy. Their bones do not develop properly and fracture easily, because of the lack of calcium. Kittens have a higher demand for this mineral than most adult cats, simply because they are growing. Unless action is taken to correct this dietary imbalance, by adding other ingredients to the diet, kittens are likely to end up permanently handicapped.

Administering vitamin D, in the form of cod liver oil, will simply worsen the condition. It is not a failure of the body to absorb sufficient calcium or to utililze the mineral. There is simply not enough available to meet the kitten's metabolic demands. Treatment necessitates supplementing the diet with adequate calcium, to ensure a calcium: phosphorus ratio of about 1:1, rather than a figure as high as 1:20, if the cat's diet consists of minced meat alone.

BELOW

A veterinarian giving a capsule. Medication can sometimes be disguised in food, but many cats are able to detect tablets here, and simply leave the medicine on the plate.

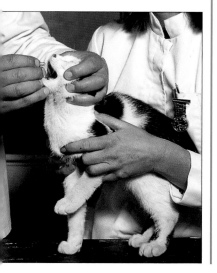

THE SPECIAL NEEDS OF KITTENS

BELOW

In spite of popular mythology, cats do not need milk to remain in good health. In actual fact, some cats, notably pedigree breeds such as the Siamese, may lack the necessary enzyme to digest the milk sugar, and will suffer from diarrhoea after drinking it. Special lactose-free milks are now available for this reason.

THE USE OF SUPPLEMENTS

There is an inter-relationship between various minerals, and there is some evidence that excessive levels of phosphorus in a cat's diet can result in kidney damage. Yet over-supplementation with calcium can also be harmful, since it is likely to depress the absorption of both zinc and magnesium from the intestinal tract into the body.

STERILIZED BONEMEAL

Aside from giving a cat a good variety of fresh foods, you must also take care to ensure that any dietary supplements are used strictly in accordance with the manufacturer's recommendations. Sterilized bonemeal has been a traditional source of additional calcium, being mixed with the cat's food. An eighth of a teaspoonful is usually added to 250 g (8 oz) of cooked food: this must be the sterilized form, rather than ordinary bonemeal used for garden fertilizer.

BONES

In the wild, of course, cats would receive calcium in their diet from the bones of their prey, where this mineral is stored. Although whole bones rarely cause problems, there is always a risk that a cat could swallow a fragment of bone which then becomes stuck in its throat. For this reason, it is not usually recommended that cats be given bones, particularly those in fish, which can be very sharp. A chicken carcass can be minced up and divided into portions for storage in a deep freezer. They can then be thawed out as required, and added to the cat's regular food. In this way, your pet will derive benefit from the mineral content of the carcass, without the risks associated with feeding bones.

Some cats appear to enjoy gnawing large marrow bones, in a similar way to dogs, but this is likely to be of more benefit to their teeth than their diet. Accumulations of food between the teeth can trigger gum disease, and providing a chew of some kind will help to prevent the build-up of plaque.

BELOW
Care must be taken with bones, especially those of fish or poultry, which can be sharp and may stick in the cat's throat if swallowed.

There are now many supplements available for cats, the majority of which contain more than one ingredient. A cod liver oil supplement will provide all three of the fat-soluble vitamins, but beware: overdosage with this group of vitamins over a period of time is inevitably harmful.

The effects of an excess of vitamin A in a high-liver diet have already been mentioned; obviously, the use of a supplement containing vitamin A would then exacerbate the situation. Before using any supplement, you need to consider the diet you are already feeding your cat and try to select a supplement to suit it, seeking veterinary advice if necessary.

The fat-soluble vitamins are stored in the liver. Specific problems can arise from overdosage, with excess vitamin E affecting blood-clotting, while too much vitamin D will lead to the build-up of calcium in the circulatory system.

This is in contrast to the situation with regard to the water-soluble vitamins, which are not stored in the body. As a result, there appears to be no risk of overdosing with them. Many diets offered to cats, especially those relying on fresh foods, are likely to be deficient in vitamin B. It is possible to supplement the diet quite easily, with yeast-based tablets, which most cats find very palatable and will take as a treat, or with a similar powder which is sprinkled on their food. Cats do not need to be given vitamin C, as they can manufacture this vitamin in their bodies.

CHOOSING THE RIGHT SUPPLEMENTS

FRESH FOODS: HOW MUCH, HOW OFTEN?

It can be difficult to assess the amount of fresh food required by your cat in the first instance, especially by a kitten because its appetite is likely to be quite large relative to its size. It is much better to overfeed rather than underfeed a kitten, to avoid stunting its growth. As a guide, young kittens need approximately three times as much food as an adult in terms of their body weight. A kitten at 10 weeks old may already be eating 190 g (7 oz) of fresh food a day. Lactating queens also require a raised intake of food.

In the case of an adult cat, you will need to offer on average every day between 140–190 g (5–7 oz) of cooked meat or fish and a further 30–60 g (1–2 oz) of rice or similar cooked carbohydrate, with a little fat being added to the diet as well. When using fresh foods, it is important to decide upon the number of feeds to be given each day, and divide the daily ration accordingly. You cannot feed on an *ad libitum* basis, since the food is liable to deteriorate during the day and will attract flies in hot weather.

Young kittens need to be fed three times a day, in the morning, at mid-day and in the evening, but as they grow older, the mid-day feed can be cut out. Indeed, some owners feed their cat only once a day, but this is less advisable when you are using fresh food.

Cats tend to be fairly fussy eaters at the best of times and, unlike dogs, do not gulp down their food at one sitting. Indeed, studies have shown that when food is constantly available, they will eat small quantities every two hours or so, around the clock.

If you leave fresh food in a warm environment for too long, it will inevitably spoil, although this may not be immediately apparent. If your cat eats food which has become contaminated by bacteria, and subsequently falls ill, it is likely to refuse this type of food in the future, although it may well be very hungry. This needs to be borne in mind, and although not every meal will have to be cooked freshly for your pet, you should provide only a small quantity in the first instance, offering a little more when this is eaten. By this means, you can be certain that the cat is receiving food which will not have deteriorated.

ABOVE
Kittens require more food that an adult cat, as do lactating queens. Food should be constantly available to both.

Many owners who prefer to feed their cats with meat, fish and similar items will prepare a week's rations at a time. The food can then be weighed up into appropriate portions, placed in plastic bags and stored in the deep-freeze until required.

It must be allowed to thaw out thoroughly before being fed to the cat, and its palatability improved by heating up a little gravy or cooking juices. It is a simple matter to mix the food and warm liquid together before giving it to your pet.

HERBS AND VEGETABLES IN THE DIET

A good variety of herbs and vegetables give extra value to a cat's food.

CARROTS

Although cats cannot convert the carotene precursor of vitamin A present in carrots to the active form of this vitamin, carrots can be of particular value following a digestive upset. They may help to regularize bowel activity, following a period of diarrhoea for example, which is likely to result in subsequent constipation (or vice-versa). Chopped into small pieces, carrots can easily be added to mince for cats.

CELERY

Celery (*Apium graveolens*) grows wild in various parts of the world, but the cultivated form is usually preferred because its taste is less bitter. It acts as a tonic, and may encourage your cat's appetite, in addition to having a diuretic action on the kidneys. Celery should be chopped up into small pieces before being added to the cat's food. One of the advantages of using mince is that herbs can be added and disguised in it more easily than if other, more solidly textured forms of meat, such as lights (pig lungs) are used.

Fresh celery stores well, for several weeks at least, if kept in a cool spot away from sunlight. It can also be grown in a garden without too much difficulty.

ABOVE
Comfrey (*Symphytum officinale*). May assist in healing of fractured bones.

COMFREY

Comfrey (*Symphytum officinale*) is valued both for its nutritional value – it has a protein content which may approach 35 per cent – and also for its medicinal qualities. Fresh leaves chopped up on the food will also provide vitamin B12.

DANDELION

Dandelion (*Taraxacum officinale*) may be a common weed, but it is also a very valuable plant. Even if you do not have a garden, you can ensure a regular supply by digging up part of a root and planting it in a pot or tub. If set just below the surface it should soon start to sprout. Alternatively, dandelion can be grown easily from seed. The leaves are a valuable source of various vitamins, including vitamin B. Dandelion can act as a slight laxative, and may encourage a cat's appetite, if this is jaded.

PARSLEY

Fresh parsley (*Petroselinum crispum*), which can be grown at home from seed, is ideal. It is a good idea to deep-freeze parsley leaves. Simply pick the required quantity, wash and shake dry, before transferring the leaves, with a little stalk attached, to freezer bags.

Storing the parsley in a freezer has an additional advantage which becomes apparent when you come to use the herb. Fresh parsley must be chopped up with a knife before being added to the cat's food. Frozen parsley can be crushed with a rolling pin.

Parsley has long been valued as a herb, with its beneficial properties being recognized by the ancient Greeks. It was widely used in Roman times for sauces and in salads. A valuable source of vitamin C, parsley can act as an appetite stimulant. It also has mild diuretic properties, making it particularly useful for older cats, as well as those which may be susceptible to feline urological syndrome (FUS, see page 46), as it helps to prevent an accumulation of uric acid in the body.

ABOVE
Parsley (*Petroselinum crispum*).
May act as an appetite
stimulant.

STINGING NETTLE

Stinging nettles (*Urtica dioica*) are a particularly valuable source of minerals including calcium, iron and manganese. They may also serve as a diuretic and laxative in the case of constipation. The young shoots may be cooked like spinach, and then chopped, by which stage they can be mixed with other foods and fed safely to cats. In addition, the liquid left after the nettles have been strained, can be cooled and used to soothe flea bites and other areas of itchy skin.

LEFT
Stinging Nettles *(Urtica dioica)*.
Valued for combating internal
haemorrhaging.

Watercress (*Nasturtium officinale*) can be used in a similar way to parsley. Use bought watercress, because watercress gathered from waterways may be contaminated. This herb is a very valuable source of vitamins and minerals, and it can be offered either fresh or cooked with the cat's food. Cooked watercress may be more palatable, as fresh watercress does have a fairly strong peppery taste.

WATERCRESS

HERBAL SUPPLEMENTS

While it may not be as easy to maintain a supply of fresh herbs during the winter months, you can augment these with herbal supplements. An increasing number of such products, specially prepared for pets, are sold in health food stores and pet shops. These may be in the form of tablets, as with comfrey, or available as a powder, as in a parsley and watercress combination, for example. If you find giving tablets to your cat difficult, it may be possible to crush them and sprinkle the powder over the cat's food.

Some fresh herbal items are distinctly seasonal, perhaps none more so than berries. Elderberries, for example, are available in the autumn, being borne on wide bracts. They are not generally difficult to harvest, because elder (*Sambucus nigra*) is a shrub which does not grow to a great height.

The elderberries change in colour from green to rich purple as they ripen, and then the whole head of berries should be cut. The berries are a great favourite of many birds, and are rapidly eaten if left too long.

Wash the berries on the stem, and then strip them off, using a fork to speed up the process. Mix just a small portion of berries with the cat's food, or extract the juice by crushing the berries in a muslin bag.

The berries also freeze well, for use at other times of the year. They are valuable sources of both iodine and iron, which is an important constituent of red blood cells. Elderberries are also said to improve the coloration of cats' coats.

ELDERBERRIES

One herbal supplement which has attracted considerable media attention during recent years has been evening primrose oil. The plant from which this is

EVENING PRIMROSE OIL

extracted is native to North America, but is now growing wild in some parts of Europe. Evening primrose (*Oenothera biennis*) is a plant of considerable medical interest, because it appears to have anti-coagulent properties, which may be of value in protecting against the development of blood clots in the circulatory system.

While this has clear applications in the field of human medicine, where it could protect against heart attacks, it could also be of direct value to cats, which can suffer from a fairly distinctive condition that is often linked to a heart infection. A blood clot, known as a thrombus, forms and is then expelled into the aorta, the major pathway for oxygenated blood leaving the heart. Where the aorta divides into the arteries supplying the hind-limbs, the thrombus is likely to become stuck, because of the reduction in diameter of the arterial system at this point.

LEFT
Evening Primrose *(Oenothera biennis)*. Can be used in a poultice for minor injuries. Carrots *(Daucus carota)*. Contain an important precursor of Vitamin A.

The use of evening primrose oil capsules could prove to be valuable in this situation, as they may assist in reducing the risk of any recurrence, as well as possibly having a preventative role, if given to cats regularly. Evening primrose oil has become valued for promoting a healthy coat, as well as improving the condition of skin. It may also assist in overcoming hormonal problems, because of its high Gamma Linoleic Acid (GLA) content, and it is sometimes combined with vitamin E as well.

FENUGREEK

Fenugreek, whose common name is an abbreviation of its scientific name, has a long history of use in herbal medicine, as well as being an important agricultural crop. It features in curries and chutney and may also be used as animal fodder, with its actions thought to include boosting the immune system to resist infections.

ABOVE
Fenugreek *(Trigonella foenum-graecum)*. May help in cases of diarrhoea.

GARLIC

Garlic has a long history of use in fighting infection. It was used in Roman times, when soldiers were given a clove of garlic daily as part of their rations. A member of the onion family, garlic grows best in the warm Mediterranean region. In addition to vitamins, it contains antibacterial substances, which help to protect against illness. It may also act on cats as a weak deworming agent.

Rather than using fresh garlic cloves, it is better to give your cat garlic tablets. These have been licensed as herbal medicines in Britain, and they assist a cat's general health as well as helping to overcome minor respiratory ailments. Garlic may also be combined with another herb, Fenugreek (*Trigonella foenum-graecum*), for treatment purposes.

RIGHT
Garlic *(Allium sativum)*. Has antibacterial properties.

KELP

One valuable product which you are likely to find only in health stores is kelp (*Fucus versiculosus*), usually sold as a powder. This seaweed is common along the shores of the north-west Atlantic, where it is found anchored to rocks. It is still collected commercially in localities as far apart as North America and the western coast of Scotland, being particularly valued as a source of iodine.

This mineral is vital for the correct functioning of the thyroid gland in the neck, which produces hormones controlling the body's metabolism and affecting its rate of activity. While iodine is also present in sea fish, supplementation is often advisable and will cause no harm. It may also have beneficial effects on the cat's coat, creating a good gloss.

ABOVE
Kelp *(Fucus vesiculosus)*. A good natural source of iodine.

TREE BARK

Tree barks can be valuable nutritional supplements. Some are available commercially, with a combination of slippery elm (*Ulmus rubra*) and poplar (*Populus candicans*) being used for weaning kittens. It can be easily mixed in either milk or water. This combination is also favoured for older cats and those convalescing from illness.

PREPARED CAT FOODS

The pet food industry has undertaken a vast amount of research to ensure that their products meet the nutritional requirements of cats, as well as being palatable. Cats have certain specific dietary needs, to the extent that dog food should not be fed to cats regularly, although if your cat occasionally steals some food from the dog bowl it will do it no harm.

TYPES OF CANNED FOODS

Canned cat foods can be divided into two basic groups. There are those that are balanced in nutritional terms, often containing flavours such as liver, and there are those that are speciality treats, containing items such as tuna, and that are not recommended for use on a regular basis. They tend to be more costly than regular diets, but reference to the labelling and the feeding instructions will clarify the position if you are in doubt. Semi-moist and dry diets are also available.

DRY CAT FOODS

Dry cat foods have some advantages over a traditional diet, in that they can be left available through the day, even in hot weather, and are unlikely to turn sour or smell unpleasant. Dry cat foods also lessen the risk of tartar accumulating on the teeth and causing gum disease and tooth decay.

PROBLEMS WITH DRIED DIETS

Dried diets have been implicated in the development of the condition known as feline urological syndrome (FUS). Crystalline material develops in the urinary tract, causing a blockage in the urethra, which carries urine from the bladder to the penis in male cats. The condition is rarer in female cats, because their urethra is both wider and shorter.

As explained later, FUS is a serious condition, which needs rapid veterinary attention. It is linked in part to reduced water intake, and dry diets contain only about 10 per cent water, whereas canned foods are made up of

70 per cent or more. Not all cats will react to a dry food diet by increasing the volume of water which they drink, to make up for this relative dietary shortage. As a result, their urine becomes reduced in volume and more concentrated, to the extent that salts may precipitate from it, creating an obstruction in the urinary tract.

Another significant factor, which once linked dried diets with FUS cases, was the level of magnesium in such foods, as was suggested by an analysis of the material which caused the blockage. This proved to be struvite, also known as magnesium ammonium phosphate. As a result, manufacturers lowered the magnesium level of their diets, to below 0.15 per cent in most cases.

Cases of FUS still occur, however, and diet alone is clearly not the cause, although it can be a contributary factor. Nor is it easy to correct the diet: it is not simply a matter of transferring a cat which has been eating dry food to a wet diet.

Indeed, the magnesium content of some fish, such as pilchards, and some meat such as beef can be about three times higher than that in a prepared canned food. The diet of a cat suffering from FUS needs to be chosen with care, to prevent the risk of any recurrence. If you decide to offer a fresh rather than a canned diet, try to avoid offering foods with a high magnesium content, at least on a regular basis.

Many vets will also recommend adding some salt to the food, stirring it in well. Three pinches per meal will be adequate to encourage your cat to drink more water. You can also pour the cooking juices, which will include the water in which the food was boiled, into the cat's feeding bowl, as a means of encouraging it to increase its fluid intake.

The amount of water which cats drink is obviously influenced by their food. On a wet diet, a cat may need to drink only around two or three tablespoons of water in order to prevent itself from becoming dehydrated. Cats have very efficient kidneys, and are also able to meet part of their fluid requirement from the metabolism of their food.

LEFT
FUS is a painful and serious condition, which requires urgent veterinary treatment. In **1** the cat is urinating normally. **2** shows the typical crouched position during urination when the cat is suffering from FUS.

LIQUID IN THE CAT'S DIET

While cats eating a dry diet have a substantially greater need for water, drinking as much as 350 ml (12 fl oz) a day, you should always ensure that fresh drinking water is available for your cat, whatever its diet. There is not necessarily any cause for alarm if it drinks less than anticipated from its water bowl. Most cats will wander outdoors, pausing to lap occasionally at puddles, ponds or other similar sources of water, and so are not totally dependent on drinking water proved for them.

There is also no real evidence to show that they prefer standing water to that poured straight from the tap, but if you have a water filter yourself for drinking water, you can pour your pet's water from the same jug and see whether it prefers it.

MILK IN THE CAT'S DIET

Many cat owners like to offer their pets milk regularly, but there should still be drinking water available at all times. Milk is not actually essential to a cat's well-being, although it will provide calcium and protein. Indeed, it can sometimes be harmful, notably in the case of the Siamese and other Oriental breeds. This is because these cats often lack the necessary digestive enzyme to break down the milk sugar, and so are likely to suffer from diarrhoea, as a result of the fermentation process which takes place in the intestines.

ABOVE
Cats must have free access to drinking water at all times, especially if they are eating dried food, when they may well drink more. It is difficult to monitor their fluid intake, however, because they may prefer drinking from other sources of water.

BELOW
The benefit of milk is that in addition to providing fluid, it also contains other ingredients, such as calcium, that can be especially valuable for growing kittens.

In other instances, cats that are unable to drink cows' milk can consume milk from goats without any adverse reaction, probably because they are allergic to the protein component of cows' milk, rather than lacking the lactase enzyme, because both forms of milk contain lactose. If this is the case, your cat may also be reluctant to sample cheese made with cows' milk as well as butter.

Such items, therefore, should not feature in its diet, although it is now possible to purchase milk which has been specially produced for lactose-intolerant cats. It is available in small packets from pet stores and can be used straight from the carton. It does not need to be refrigerated, until opened, and is generally highly palatable to cats of all ages, even if they have not been given milk regularly in the past.

ALLERGIES

The subject of allergies has been the focus of increasing attention in recent years. It is important to distinguish between a cat's inability to digest a component of food, such as lactose, and an allergy, where exposure to even the smallest quantity of the problem food will evoke an allergic reaction. This is the body's response to what it perceives to be a harmful substance, so that it reacts by producing antibodies.

No allergy to a new food can occur within less than 10 days of a cat's consuming it for the first time. This is the minimum period which it takes for the immune response to develop antibodies, following exposure to the allergen which causes the reaction.

RIGHT
Some cats, such as many Siamese, are actually allergic to milk.

INVESTIGATING THE SOURCES OF ALLERGIES

It is very difficult and time-consuming in many cases to investigate a suspected allergic condition. This is because the source of the allergy must be isolated. Your veterinarian will be able to advise you on specific details, but generally, your cat will need to be fed a very simple (but nevertheless healthy) diet, based perhaps on chicken, cooked brown rice and a small amount of vegetables, for a period of at least two months or so.

Assuming the adverse effects of the suspected allergy disappear during this stage, the next step to isolating the cause is to reintroduce other foods individually, observing the cat's reaction to them. If the previous symptoms start to recur, then you are likely to have identified the allergen successfully, although this does not yet rule out the possibility of a multiple allergy. Further investigation along these lines will be required for this purpose.

DON'T FORGET THE CAT'S ENVIRONMENT

It is important to consider that the suspected allergic reaction could have been triggered by something other than the cat's diet. It could well have been caused by an environmental factor, such as the disinfectant used to clean the kitchen floor or even the cat's bedding.

Try to examine all the possible causes and adjust the cat's exposure to them, in the hope of isolating the factor responsible. Indeed, it has been suggested that only a third of allergies are of dietary origin so it may take time to track the source. Thankfully, relatively few cats suffer from allergies.

ALLERGIC TO CATS!

In contrast, people can become sensitized to cats, especially those with long hair, a problem which can prove especially traumatic if only one member of the family is affected. Obviously, the cat should be excluded from all bedrooms, and the house should be regularly and thoroughly cleaned with a vacuum cleaner which retains almost all the dust which it collects.

Runny eyes, sneezing and a tight-chested feeling, especially after handling the cat, are all likely symptoms of an allergy, which a doctor will be able to confirm. Up to now, it has been very difficult to do anything to correct this problem, but recently in North America, trials of a vaccine have begun, which may offer real hope to those afflicted by this distressing and sad condition.

FELINE OBESITY

As a general rule, cats suffer far less from obesity than dogs, because they tend not to overeat and therefore do not put on excessive weight. Their energy expenditure is closely matched by their food intake, although on some days, if given a favoured food, they may eat more than at other times. The best guide as to whether a cat is overweight is to see whether you can feel its ribs without difficulty. If you cannot, then your cat is almost certainly obese.

The risk of obesity is greater if the cat is neutered, and it may be worthwhile reducing its food intake slightly following this surgery. The only means of maintaining an accurate check on your cat's weight is to weigh it regularly and keep a record of these figures.

RIGHT
Obesity is not usually a serious problem in cats, but it still needs to be guarded against. It will eventually cause your pet discomfort and affect its health.

WEIGHING A CAT

The simplest way to weigh a cat is to pick it up, and then stand on a set of bathroom scales, checking they are properly calibrated. Having obtained a figure, put the cat down, weigh yourself alone, and subtract this reading from the first, to give you the cat's weight.

CONTROLLING A CAT'S FOOD INTAKE

Reducing a cat's food intake is obviously the easiest means of ensuring weight loss over a period of time, but it is not so straightforward in practice. Unlike dogs, cats are highly adept at finding other sources of food if they are hungry; they may foist themselves on neighbours, take food intended for other cats or simply resort to hunting, although this latter activity may require more energy.

The most satisfactory answer is not to reduce the quantity of food, which will cause the cat to look elsewhere, but rather to reduce its nutritional value overall. This will have the effect of causing the cat to metabolize its fat stores, but without feeling hungry.

If you have been in the habit of giving the cat titbits during the day, cut them out, feeding it only at set meal times. Milk should also be replaced by water as far as possible, either by diluting it or by replacing full cream milk with a low-fat (skimmed) variety instead.

As for the diet itself, you could add items such as bran and increase the vegetable content (although not potatoes, which are a source of carbohydrate), mixing them in with the meat or fish. Kelp can also be added to the diet, since this is considered to be of value in helping to stimulate weight loss.

ABOVE
The Maine Coon, a North American breed, is one of the heaviest breeds in the world, and tends to have a correspondingly hearty appetite.

Speak to your veterinarian as well, for guidance about the target weight you are seeking to achieve for the cat. There are some variations in feline body weight, especially among the various pedigree breeds. Maine Coons are generally considered to be the heaviest domestic cat, with males weighing as much as 8 kg (18 lb). Smaller breeds are considerably lighter: the Singapura, for example, typically weighs under 2.7 kg (6 lb).

It is important to ensure that your cat does not become overweight, because not only its lifestyle but also its health with be under threat. A fat cat tends to take less exercise, and so the problem of obesity becomes exacerbated, while its food intake remains constant. Not only does this affect its general level of fitness, but should the cat need surgery for any reason, it will be at greater risk with the anaesthetic, and sutures may even split apart because of the increased body fat.

ABOVE
In contrast, the Singapura will tend to eat less, being much smaller in size. Guidelines given for feeding purposes on packs tend to be rather approximate.

LACK OF APPETITE

T he fact that a cat does not eat for a day or so need not necessarily be a cause for concern, although it could be a sign of impending illness and a close watch should be kept on it.

Factors that may cause a cat to lose its appetite temporarily include changes in its routine, such as coming home from a visit to a vet, and thunderstorms, as well as fireworks being let off, particularly while the cat is outside. If frightened, it is likely to come inside and hide, rather than eat. There is always the possibility, too, that it may have found another source of food elsewhere, preferring a neighbour's offerings to your own.

ABOVE
Fur balls are a common reason for loss of appetite in cats, because they occupy part of the stomach. Under these circumstances, a cat does not lose its appetite entirely, but continues to pick at its food.

After a period of illness, it can also be quite difficult to persuade a cat to start eating normally again. Cats rely heavily on their sense of smell to kindle their appetite, and those that have been suffering from respiratory illnesses may need to be given foods with powerful odours. Wipe the cat's nose first, if there is any discharge, before putting food in front of it.

A good food at this stage in a cat's convalescence is pilchards in tomato sauce; covering other foods with either meat extracts or gravy can also be tempting to a cat which has been poorly. You can even dab a little liquid of this type on its nose, which the cat will lick off and so will perhaps gain a taste for the food on offer. Warm food, as mentioned previously, is also more palatable. Once a cat starts eating again, its appetite should soon return to normal.

TEMPTING JADED APPETITES

THE HAZARDS OF DAILY LIFE

S ome cats are not content to rely on food provided for them, but prefer to go out hunting for their own as well. This is often a cause of distress to owners, but is quite natural behaviour. There is little that can be done to overcome a cat's hunting instincts. As a general rule, cross-bred cats, especially those reared on farms, display a stronger desire to hunt than pedigree cats, because hunting abilities are not entirely instinctive but have to be learnt. Farm cats are much more likely to come into contact with potential prey such as mice than pure-bred kittens reared in a cattery.

There are risks attached to hunting behaviour, especially when the prey is eaten. Cats will usually consume mice whole, swallowing them head first, although they tend not to digest the fur. A number of parasites rely on rodents for part of their life cycle, which is then

ABOVE
In spite of popular mythology, cats rarely become trapped up trees; even though they may be driven up here by a pursuing dog, they are normally capable of finding their own way back down, if left undisturbed.

completed when the cat consumes the rodent. Both tapeworms and roundworms can be spread to cats by this route, and may also be present in other creatures sometimes eaten by cats, ranging from earthworms to birds. Regular deworming is to be recommended for all cats, but assumes particular importance in the case of those which hunt regularly.

Feline lungworm (*Aelurostrongylus alstrusus*) is another, more serious parasitic infection acquired in the same way. In urban areas, cats are particularly susceptible to these parasitic ailments, which typically occur at a high density. This means that the risk of such infections being spread to other creatures which act as so-called intermediate hosts is correspondingly increased, as is the likelihood of cats then encountering the infections again subsequently, unless all owners in the area regularly deworm their pets.

LIFE CYCLE OF A LUNGWORM

The adult lungworm lives in the lungs of cats (**1**). It lays eggs in the air passages, which are then coughed up and develop into larvae which are passed out in the motions (**2**). The eggs lie on the ground, until they are ingested by a molluscan intermediate host such as a snail (**3**). It is thought that these infected molluscs are then eaten by birds (**4**), which are then in turn eaten by cats (**5**).

POISONING

Another less obvious problem of hunting in the town is that rodenticides may have been laid here. Affected rats or mice often present relatively easy targets for cats, who themselves may then be affected by the poison. Warfarin, which interferes with the blood clotting mechanism, causing internal haemorrhaging, represents a particular hazard for cats. Unlike dogs, they typically will not eat the bait itself, but can still succumb by consuming rodents suffering from warfarin poisoning.

Unfortunately, this exposure is not always apparent until it is too late. Typical symptoms may include frothing around the mouth and nose, weakness, difficulty in breathing and a characteristic pallor of the mucous membranes on the inside of the mouth.

Sudden death is likely to result in more serious cases. If you have reason to suspect warfarin poisoning, you should seek veterinary help without delay. Treatment may then be possible. It involves administering vitamin K, intravenously with a dextrose solution initially, and then in tablet form for a further six days, once the cat's recovery is under way.

One poison which a cat may find sufficiently appealing to consume is metaldehyde. This was frequently used as a snail and slug killer in gardens, but is now less commonly encountered, because of concern about the safety of pets and wildlife. An affected cat may froth at the mouth and display signs of weakness, before losing consciousness. Death in this case is usually due to respiratory failure.

Metaldehyde poisoning can result in complications such as liver damage, with treatment being difficult. It relies on removing the chemical as far as possible from the cat's body by giving an emetic, often followed by respiratory support on a ventilator and anaesthesia to control convulsions.

URBAN HAZARDS

Not all substances which prove fatal to cats are typically used as poisons, and cats are more likely to come across them with greater frequency in urban areas. A particular hazard is anti-freeze, stored in many garages. Many cats find the taste of the chemical ethylene glycol, which is the major ingredient, very appealing and will lap it up readily.

Unfortunately, once in the body, the ethylene glycol is converted to deadly oxalic acid, which crystallizes out in the kidneys and results in death from renal failure. As with other poisons, the key to ensuring your cat's survival is to seek the help of a veterinarian without

delay, should you suspect that your pet might have been poisoned. If it has, it is likely to be seen staggering, before collapsing and convulsing. Treatment entails the administration of ethanol, although occasionally, where the renal damage is severe, a kidney transplant has been carried out to save a cat's life.

POISONOUS PLANTS

It is not just outside the home that the cat's appetite for harmful substances may manifest itself. Some house-plants, including ivies, dumb cane (*Dieffenbachia*) and poinsettias, are liable to be poisonous if consumed. Mistletoe, brought into the home at Christmas, can also be harmful.

Cats housed permanently indoors are more likely to nibble houseplants than those which can roam outdoors as well. By way of compensation, they should always be offered a pot of grass which they can chew, while potentially harmful plants should be kept in bedrooms or other places where they will be out of the cat's reach.

RIGHT
Some popular garden plants that are poisonous and your cat should avoid are: *Iris* (**1**), Ivy, *Hedera* (**2**), Cornflower, *Centaura* (**3**), Bird of Paradise, *Strelitzia* (**4**), Christmas Rose, *Heleborus* (**5**), Laburnum (**6**). Foxglove, *Digitalis* (**7**), and Yew, *Taxus* (**8**).

ABOVE
Some chemicals used in the garden, such as slug pellets containing metaldehyde, are liable to be poisonous if eaten by a cat. Cats often eat grass to relieve blockages caused by fur balls, or to clear out worms. The cat will vomit up both.

Some pet shops sell containers with grass seed, which simply need to be watered and left to germinate, especially for cats, which prefer fresh green shoots. A container of grass should have longer stems cut down before they become coarse, and the soil is kept moist. The reasons why cats eat grass occasionally are various. It may be to compensate for any deficiency of folic acid, a member of the group of B vitamins, in their diet. Grass may also serve to provide necessary bulk and roughage, which could be lacking in a prepared diet.

When a cat wishes to be sick, it will also consume grass, often preferring coarser strands in this situation. It may do this to relieve a blockage resulting from a fur ball in its stomach, or sometimes may even be using it as an emetic to clear parasitic worms from its tract. These will be vomited up with the grass, soon after the grass has been eaten. Some preliminary retching may give you enough warning to be able to carry your cat outside in time. You should obtain a deworming preparation from your vet to prevent any recurrence.

CATS AND GRASS

Another problematical habit among cats is the way in which they drag their food out of their bowl, disappearing with it into another part of the house. It is behaviour often associated with cats of a relatively nervous disposition, and can usually be overcome by readjusting their feeding routine.

Such behaviour also stems from the cat's wild instincts. Having caught prey, cats invariably drag or carry it off to a quiet locality where they can eat undisturbed. In the first instance, you can make this difficult by ensuring the cat's food is finely minced, so that pieces cannot be taken away easily. You should also consider where you are feeding your cat.

The kitchen is often a busy thoroughfare, giving your cat little privacy. It may simply be trying to withdraw with its food to a quieter locality. You can either move the food bowl elsewhere, so the cat can feed in relative peace, or feed your pet at a time when no other disturbances are likely to arise in the kitchen.

A QUIET PLACE TO EAT

RIGHT
Always try to feed a kitten or an older cat in a quiet area, where it can eat undisturbed. Many cats, like dogs, desire privacy when eating.

CLEANLINESS THE NATURAL WAY

3

One of the most significant aspects of taking on a new kitten is toilet training. Cats are clean creatures by nature, and by the time they are weaned, kittens will already be familiar with the need to use a dirt or litter tray, when they are not allowed outdoors. It is also helpful to know that kittens will often relieve themselves after a meal, so that placing a kitten on its litter tray when it has finished eating can have the desired result, and it will soon learn to return to it of its own accord.

ABOVE
A basic litter tray.

LITTER TRAYS

The litter tray should be positioned in a quiet place where the young cat will not be disturbed. A liner in the litter tray will help to keep it clean, and there are various herbal products available to help prevent unpleasant smells, although, obviously, these are no substitute for regular cleaning.

CAT LITTER

Various substances are marketed as cat litter, with those manufactured from clay being perhaps the most widely used. Most of these will clump together effectively when wet, so that soiled litter can be removed quite easily, with minimum waste. Other types of litter are based on compacted wood, sold in a pelleted form. Loose sawdust or shavings are not to be recommended, because they can be scattered easily outside the litter tray, and pieces may become stuck in the cat's fur, especially if it is long-haired.

Peat is equally messy, and using it as cat litter is rather wasteful of a precious resource, when there are other, better choices available. Garden soil may be used as an alternative, but it is messy and less hygienic, and is liable to stick to the cat's paws when wet.

RIGHT
Cats are most likely to want to use a litter tray after waking up, or following a meal. Be sure that the litter is clean – otherwise, the cat may disregard it.

DISPOSING OF DIRTY LITTER

While it may seem a good idea simply to discard soiled cat litter on to a garden refuse heap, this is not to be recommended, because you could simply be spreading parasites, notably roundworm eggs and especially the protozoal cysts of *Toxoplasma*. These are very resistant to decay, and ultimately could end up being scattered on the flowerbeds, representing a risk not only to cats in the neighbourhood, but also, in the case of *Toxoplasma gonadii*, to pregnant women. *Toxoplasma* can cross the placenta, resulting in miscarriages in women who have not previously been exposed to the parasite. Gardening gloves should always be worn as a precaution in any event, in case other cats have used the garden for their toilet.

The best way to dispose of soiled cat litter is to tie it up in a plastic bag, and dispose of it along with the rest of the household refuse. Flushing the contents of the litter tray down the toilet is definitely not to be recommended.

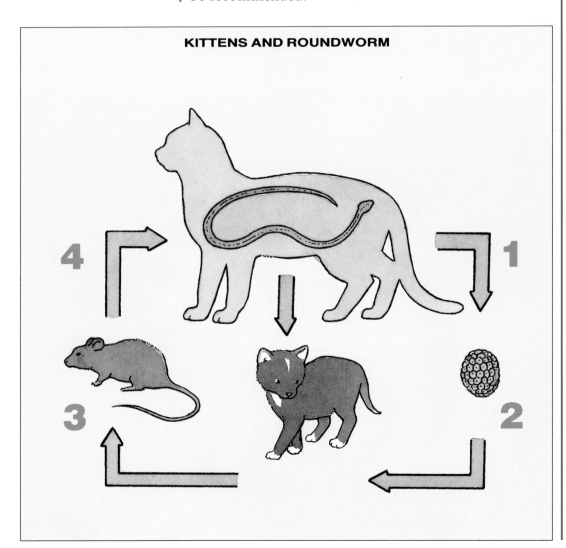

KITTENS AND ROUNDWORM

LEFT
Ascarid roundworms grow in the intestines of a cat (**1**) and feed on the digested food there. Their eggs (**2**) are passed on via faeces, which may be swallowed by another cat, and if this happens, the larvae hatch in its intestines. The danger to a newborn kitten is that the larval stage of the *Toxocara cati* species migrate to the mother's milk at the onset of lactation and infect the kitten (**3**). Alternatively, the eggs of either of the known species of roundworm, *Toxocara cati* or *Toxocascaris leonina*, in the faeces may be eaten by another animal – such as a beetle, bird, rat or mouse (**4**) – that a cat may prey upon and so in turn infect the cat.

GROOMING

Although cats will spend long periods grooming themselves, they will benefit from being groomed by their owners, too. A range of equipment is available for the purpose; brushes are particularly useful in removing dead hair from the coat, while combs will ensure that there are no tangles. Long-haired cats are especially prone to matting of their coats if they are not groomed every day. This can lead on to other problems such as fly strike, if left unchecked, a condition resulting from flies laying eggs in soiled fur and eggs hatching, setting up a toxic reaction which can be fatal.

It is a good idea to accustom kittens to being groomed regularly, even though their coats are less profuse than an adult cat's. Grooming also provides the opportunity to look for parasites, notably fleas, which may otherwise remain relatively inconspicuous, while causing the cat great irritation.

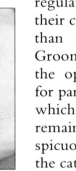

BELOW
Careful grooming will enable you to detect troublesome parasites, such as fleas, as well as removing moulted hairs from the cat's coat before these are swallowed, possibly resulting in fur balls.

ABOVE
The sharp spines on the cat's tongue are clearly visible in this photograph. They help the cat to swallow its prey head first, and also pull out loose hairs when grooming its coat.

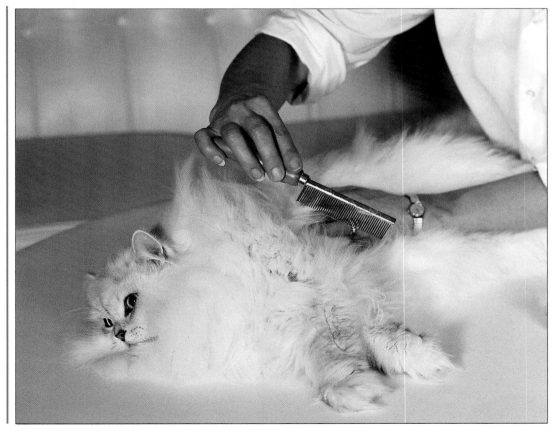

DEALING WITH FLEAS

Grooming is best carried out outdoors if you suspect that your cat has fleas. A fine-toothed flea comb will confirm their presence, even if you do not see these troublesome parasites, and will even catch a few of them. Look for tiny blackish-red specks among the fur on the comb; these are likely to be flea dirt, containing traces of undigested blood. You can confirm this by moistening them on a white sheet of paper: a red deposit will develop if it is flea dirt.

Fleas are most likely to be found towards the base of the tail and over the hindquarters, although they may occur anywhere in the fur. They are very agile, and the easiest means of destroying any found while grooming your cat is to drop them into a container of water.

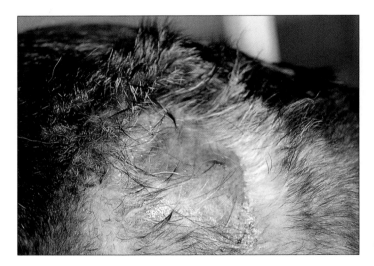

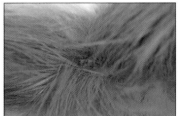

LEFT
The presence of fleas will cause a cat to scratch itself more than usual, with the resulting flea bites sometimes becoming infected, and developing into large sores.

LEFT
Fleas represent a hazard to people too, biting when they are hungry, although there is no risk of cat fleas living permanently on a person.

ABOVE
Here the flea bite has become infected, and requires additional treatment. Over a period of time, cats can also become sensitised to flea saliva, and develop a flea bite allergy, with just a single bite causing them great discomfort.

It is very important to kill fleas, because not only will their biting distress your cat, but there is also a real risk that the cat could become sensitized to their saliva, giving rise to a condition sometimes described as "flea bite allergy". Fleas can also be the intermediate host for tapeworm, with the cat becoming infected when it consumes the flea, which it may do inadvertently when it grooms itself. Treatment for tapeworm is often recommended after a severe flea infestation.

The aim should be to prevent the cat suffering from fleas as far as possible. Partly as a result of concerns over the chemicals contained within traditional flea collars, there has been a move towards incorporating more natural remedies into them. Since cats often spend much of their time climbing around, it is vital that a flea collar (or indeed any collar) should be elasticated. Then if it becomes caught on a branch, the cat can wriggle free without difficulty and not strangle itself inadvertantly.

TRANSMISSION OF A VIRUS

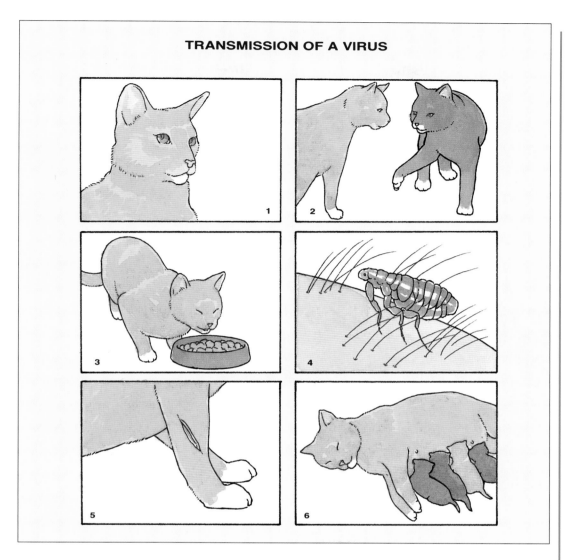

There are several ways that a virus may spread from cat to cat. It may be airborne (**1**), in droplets that are coughed or sneezed, as in the transmission of cat 'flu. Some of the more resistant viruses such as feline panleucopaenia may simply be transmitted on contact (**2**) or indirectly on contaminated items such as bedding, grooming implements and feeding bowls. Feline panleucopaenia is also an example of a virus that is transmitted by being ingested in food and swallowed (**3**). Other kinds of diseases are spread by bites from insects or other animals (**4**). Open cuts and wounds are another way of transmitting a virus (**5**). A particular danger to developing kittens is that some viruses are small enough to pass across the placenta, or contaminate the mother's milk and infect newborn kittens (**6**).

A variety of herbs known to act as flea repellents have been incorporated into collars. It is possible to re-use some of these collars by immersing them in the recommended herbal solution, rather than simply discarding them after a set period of time.

RIGHT
If you use a flea collar, you will need to be sure that it is elasticated, to prevent any risk of your cat becoming entangled by it. In addition, check that it does not provoke any skin reaction.

Certain aromatic herbal powders can also be applied to the cat's coat; as always, read the accompanying instructions carefully. Cats are especially vulnerable to the effects of anything applied to their coats, because they spend long periods licking their fur, and so can ingest the active ingredients.

Pennyroyal (*Mentha pulegium*), a form of mint, has a long history of combating fleas on people as well as animals. The plant grows quite easily in most parts of the world, with the American pennyroyal (*Hedeoma pulegioides*) seeming to have identical properties to its Old World relative.

Eucalyptus (*Eucalyptus globulus*) is also another aromatic plant, in this case a tree, which is often incorporated in herbal flea remedies. Wormwood (*Artemisia absinthium*), rosemary (*Rosmarinus officinalis*) and rue (*Ruta graveolens*) are other herbs considered of value in the fight against fleas.

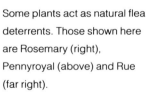

Some plants act as natural flea deterrents. Those shown here are Rosemary (right), Pennyroyal (above) and Rue (far right).

It is always important to treat not just the cat, but also its environment, because flea eggs accumulate here, rather than on the cat. Bedding must be washed regularly, and vacuuming the cat's sleeping area will also help to remove microscopic flea eggs before they can hatch.

A chalk-like substance produced from fossilized algae and marketed as diatomaceous earth, also offers a means of combating fleas directly in the home. It is harmless to animals, as well as people, but will destroy the fleas by damaging their body casing.

While fleas tend to be a particular problem in late summer, plagues can arise at other times of the year, especially in centrally heated houses.

It is important to soothe the skin of a cat suffering from flea bites. If your pet continues scratching the affected areas, there is an increasing risk of local infections developing and spreading across damaged areas of skin. Lemon juice, suitably diluted, can be soothing. Simply slice up a lemon, and add it to 600 ml (1 pt) of warm water, leaving the solution to stand for approximately 12 hours. Then bathe the affected area with the solution applied on cotton-wool.

Never apply undiluted herbal oils direct to a cat's skin, because this may well result in further irritation.

RIGHT
It is possible to make some soothing remedies quite easily at home. This one entails lemon and water.

BATHING A CAT You may need to bathe your cat with a suitable shampoo to kill fleas. This can be a rather difficult task, because many cats dislike being in water – although the Turkish Van breed does appear to have a natural affinity for it.

BELOW
Most cats are not keen on being bathed, but can become accustomed to the experience. Be sure to keep any shampoo out of the eyes and ears, and avoid wetting the head until last. Cats generally find this the most upsetting part of the procedure.

A sink is perhaps the best place to bath a cat, particularly if you can attach a shower fitment to the taps. You may want to wear a pair of reasonably stout gloves for protection in case your cat is one of the many which actively resent being bathed. Try to make things as organized as possible from the outset, having the shampoo and towels to hand, with a firm base, such as a rubber mat, in the sink so the cat can retain its grip in the water easily. You may want to block off the cat's ears with cotton-wool before you start, so that no water can get in by accident.

Fill the sink with tepid

ABOVE
A Turkish Van cat in water. This breed is unique in that it appears to actively enjoy swimming.

water. You can then wet the cat's fur, scooping the water up with your hands; alternatively, simply stand the cat in the basin, and wet its coat using a shower attachment. Some cats find this less disturbing, but be sure not to use water which is anything other than tepid, because their skin is very sensitive.

The simplest means of restraining the cat is to press down on the scruff of the neck. Be sure that you are aware of the instructions for using the shampoo, especially the length of time it has to be left on the coat, before being washed off. Rub it gently over the body, leaving the head until the last. It is very important that the shampoo does not get into the cat's eyes, as this will cause it considerable distress.

Similarly, take care when rinsing the shampoo out of the coat, and allow as much water to drain out as possible, before wrapping the cat in a towel and lifting it out of the basin. It is important to dry the fur well. Some cats will allow you to use a hairdrier, but the setting should not be too high, and the warm air should be kept away from the head as far as possible.

Do not let the cat go outside straight after a bath, but wait until the fur has dried completely so that it will not become chilled. You must also bear in mind that unless the cat's environment has been thoroughly treated against fleas, it is almost certain that your pet will succumb again, as further flea eggs start to hatch.

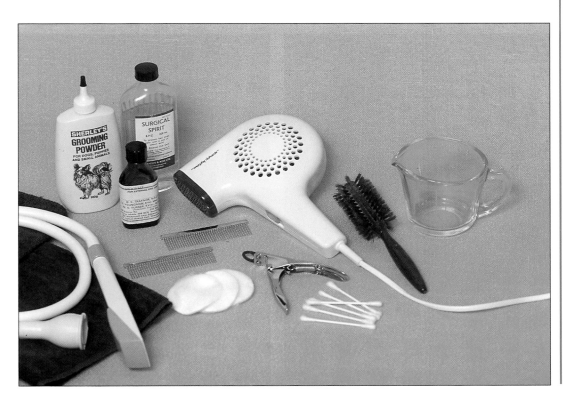

LEFT
A variety of cat bathing and grooming equipment is available, and is useful for the care of both pet and show cats.

The typical behaviour of a cat afflicted by a fur ball looks at first sight like loss of appetite. The cat eats less than normal and seems to be fussy about its food, while at the same time appearing hungry. It darts back and forth to the food bowl, consuming small quantities.

This behaviour relates directly to the solid pad of the fur ball obstruction in its stomach. There is a risk that the accumulation of hair could cause a blockage in the intestines, should it pass out of the stomach. Liquid paraffin is given as a laxative, to assist the passage of the fur ball through the tract and out of the body, while not being absorbed itself. If the fur ball is relatively small, the cat may be able to vomit it out of its stomach.

NAILS

Cat's claws are best cut with a stout pair of clippers. Those of the guillotine-type, incorporating a sliding blade, are easiest to use, as there is less chance of cutting the nail too short. It is important to locate the blood supply – visible as a thin red streak – before cutting the nail.

OPPOSITE

With the right amount of attention from its owner, any cat should be able to enjoy life, indoors and outdoors in good health.

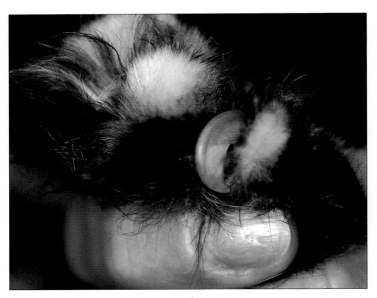

ABOVE

The nails of the cat are kept sharp by scratching, and are not just used for hunting but also for climbing. If the cat does not walk on a hard surface, then its claws are likely to become overgrown, and will need to be clipped.

ABOVE

An ingrown nail is shown here. This has become too long and is twisting into the pad. If it is not cut, then it may actually penetrate the pad, causing a great deal of pain.

HEALTH CARE

4

While you will obviously need veterinary assistance if your cat falls ill, there is much that you can do yourself, in terms of nursing care, to help your pet through illness and speed its recovery. The signs of illness are often clear-cut, with loss of appetite, lethargy, vomiting, diarrhoea and discharges, coughing and physical weakness or disability all likely indicators of a potential problem.

When consulting your vet, you should provide as detailed a history as possible, and follow the treatment instructions with the greatest care. Details concerning dosage of tablets and other medications will be given on their labelling. There may be accompanying instructions about withholding food for a period after administering the tablet; this is quite usual practice with homoeopathic treatments.

DOSAGE

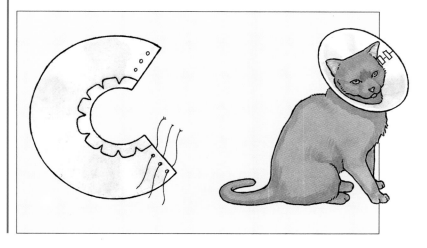

Although cats are generally very healthy, they can be prone to respiratory infections. In such situations, bathing a cat's nose to remove any secretions will not only assist its recovery but also encourage its appetite. There are various soothing agents which you can apply to prevent soreness and assist the healing process. Almond oil, gently rubbed on the nose two or three times a day, is one such. Another is calendulated oil, made up by stirring a couple of drops of calendula tincture into 25 ml/1 fl oz of olive oil.

HELP FOR RESPIRATORY INFECTIONS

Olive oil is also useful for cleaning a cat's ears, breaking down any accumulation of wax. Warm the oil first, so that it flows more freely, by standing a small glass jar of the oil in a container of hot water. Then carefully run about a teaspoonful into each ear in turn. Start by gently tilting the cat's head on one side, so that you have a clear view of the ear canal. Using a spoon, the sides of which have been bent upwards to form a funnel, makes applying the oil easier. Allow it to trickle slowly down into the ear. Do not rush the procedure, because the oil will simply run down the sides of the cat's face, rather than into the ear.

WAX IN THE EARS

Gently massage the ear from behind and below, and after a short time you should be able to detect a change in consistency, indicating that the wax has been broken down. A cotton-wool bud can be used very carefully to absorb the waxy debris, taking care not to poke the bud into the ear canal, which could be painful. If the ear appears very sore, calendulated oil (see above) may be used for its soothing properties.

ABOVE
Ear drops can be administered quite easily, especially if there is someone else holding the cat for you, while you put the medication into the ear.

LEFT
An accumulation of ear wax may contain bacteria, mites and fungi, all of which can cause ear infections. A cat with an ear infection may scratch repeatedly at the ear, and resent this area of the body being touched.

SOOTHING SORE EYES

The cat's eyes may also be affected in a case of respiratory disease; they are often also injured in fights. A mild solution of salt, made by dissolving half a teaspoonful of sea salt in 600 ml (1 pt) of distilled water, can be used initially to bathe the eyes, applying the solution on cotton-wool.

Alternatively, the salt solution can be boiled and then used to form a herbal infusion, by adding a heaped teaspoonful of eyebright *(Euphrasia rostkoviana)* to a cup of the solution. Allow it to cool before applying it to the cat's eyes, up to three times a day. Provided that it is covered and small quantities tipped into a separate container, this infusion will remain fresh for a day.

ABOVE
Eye drops should be given carefully with a special dropper, to ensure that the medication is not lost from the eyes.

LEFT
Infected eyes should be bathed carefully, with particular attention being paid to the corners close to the nose, where the majority of debris is likely to accumulate. This treatment may need to be repeated several times daily.

SKIN PROBLEMS

M ale cats, in particular, are prone to fight, and may continue to do so even after they are neutered. They are often bitten in fights, while females can also be bitten. The result of a bite is often an abscess forming at the site of the bite. The sudden appearance of an abscess can be very alarming, especially as the puncture wounds in the first instance are often inconspicuous enough to go unnoticed.

The cat's owner probably first sees a swelling, often on the side of the face, which increases rapidly in size. This results from bacteria being effectively injected into the cat's body by the opponent's bite. The skin then heals quite rapidly, and the abscess, which will be full of pus, starts to develop.

An abscess cannot be cured quickly. It should be allowed to come to a head and then burst. At first, the cat may lose its appetite, particularly if the bite is on the head, while the abscess itself will feel hot to the touch.

Vitamin C, in the form of 250 mg tablets, given three times a day over the course of three days, can help to boost the cat's immune system. The use of *Ledum*, especially with *Hypericum,* and given three times daily over the course of two days, starting out with one tablet every two hours on the first day, is typically recommended in such cases. The potency used varies from 6c to 200c.

As the abscess becomes ready to burst, *Hepar sulphuris* can speed the process, initially given at a potency of 6c, which can be increased to 200c for healing purposes. In addition, tincture of calendula, prepared using one quarter of a teaspoonful to a cup of hot distilled water, and sponged on to the abscess twice daily, will also bring relief.

While many abscesses will heal uneventfully, there can be complications, giving rise to a more chronic infection. This may be prevented by the use of *Silicea*, at a potency of 200c, being used three times a week over a month. It is advisable to prevent the drainage holes from healing prematurely, before all the pus has been drained out; bathing helps prevent the holes from healing. Wiping the skin area with hydrogen peroxide should help to ensure successful healing.

RIGHT
An abscess on a cat's head, incurred as the result of a fight.

RODENT ULCER

It used to be thought that this condition was somehow caught by cats from rodents, but the precise cause has not yet been established. Rodent ulcers typically occur on the upper lip and may extend towards the nose, although they can occur elsewhere in the mouth. The affected area is brownish and tends to create an irregular profile along the lip, with the edge rolling over where it is affected.

Treatment is invariably difficult, though *Kali bi-chromicum*, at a potency of 200c, has been known to give good results. The lesion itself appears to cause the cat relatively little discomfort. A single dose given three times a week for a period of six weeks may be required to cure the ulcer.

MILIARY ECZEMA

A skin problem which can arise after neutering, especially in female cats, is miliary eczema. Hormonal treatment will be required, with folliculinum being favoured for females. The usual recommendation is a 6c dose twice a day for three weeks; after an interval of a week, recommence with a 30c potency, given three times a week for a month. Relapses may occur and the characteristic pimply rashes may return, most notably along the back. The treatment should then be repeated.

Testosterone is the chosen remedy for male cats suffering from the condition, with similar potencies being used, although results are sometimes less encouraging.

The cause of other skin ailments in cats may be less clear-cut, but your vet will be able to carry out tests, following a skin scraping of the affected area, to try to ascertain the cause. Sometimes, skin disorders can be linked to the cat's diet. Again, sulphur may prove a valuable remedy, with calendula ointment helping to relieve any irritation.

In spite of its name, this is a fungal rather than a parasitic ailment, and is of particular concern in that it is a zoonosis – that is, a disease transmissible to people. Ringworm lesions are often very inconspicuous in cats, in contrast to cattle, for example, on which the circular patches caused by the fungus are very evident, being paler than the rest of the coat.

It is at the proximity of the lesion that there is the greatest concentration of fungal spores. Two different forms of fungus may be implicated in cases of feline ringworm, of which *Microsporum* is far more common than *Trichophyton*. In some cases it is possible to confirm ringworm by examining the cat's coat in a darkened room using a Wood's lamp, which will cause the affected areas to fluoresce apple-green.

People can pick up ringworm without realizing it, because of a lack of clinical signs of the infection in their pet. (Red, circular patches on the arms are typically seen in cases of human ringworm.) Close examination of the cat may then reveal slight hair loss, often on the head. Should this not fluoresce, your vet will be able to arrange for cultures to be made, to detect any fungus.

Care needs to be taken because the fungal spores survive well in the environment. Thorough cleaning of the cat's quarters is essential, bedding should be disposed of and, ideally, the cat should be kept confined until treatment is completed. This will take at least a month, and possibly longer.

A suitable homoeopathic treatment is *Trichophyton* and *Microsporum* nosodes in a combined form, at a 30c potency. The dose needs to be given weekly, for a period of six weeks, while the affected areas should be treated each day as advised with a solution of *Hypericum* and *Calendula* (Hypercal).

Oil of lavender painted on to the bald areas each day is recommended as a herbal treatment, and is easily applied using a brush. Wear disposable gloves when handling a cat with ringworm, and always wash your hands thoroughly, using cold rather than hot water, as it is less likely to open up your skin pores, making it harder for the fungal spores to become established and infect you.

ABOVE
A Wood's lamp in action, being used to examine a cat for evidence of ringworm. Most types of ringworm will fluoresce under this light, assisting the diagnostic process. In contrast, it can take several weeks for the fungus to grow on special media in the laboratory.

ABOVE
Signs of ringworm are clearly visible here. The most infective part of this lesion is around the perimeter, where healthy and diseased hair meet.

BELOW
A classic case of human ringworm, acquired from a cat. Circular lesions of this type should always receive medical attention. They are often on the forearm, because as the person picks the cat up, so its hair rubs against this part of the arm.

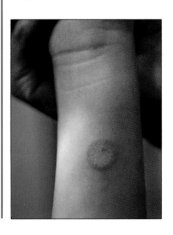

SKIN PARASITES

Cats can get a variety of mites, lice, ticks and fleas on their bodies, although the susceptibility of individual cats varies. Cats which are well fed and generally healthy are far less likely to suffer from a heavy infestation of lice, although the cat's nutritional state does not appear to affect the incidence of fleas. Ticks are most common in agricultural areas, and feed on the cat's blood.

LEFT
Ticks will swell in size as they feed on blood. It is possible to eliminate them quite easily, however.

The herbal powders recommended for the treatment of fleas (see page 64) will control these other parasites as well. In the case of ticks, the simplest method of control is not to resort to chemicals or attempt to pull off the tick, because you will inevitably leave its headparts lodged in the cat's skin, where they are likely to cause a localized infection.

Instead, simply smear the tick with petroleum jelly, especially over its rear when it has a respiratory pore. Unable to breathe, the tick will eventually let go of its own accord and fall off. Control of ticks is important, because they can be responsible for spreading blood-borne diseases in some parts of the world.

Lice can be killed quite easily using pennyroyal shampoo. They are much easier than fleas to control, because they lay their eggs on the cat's hairs, and so do not occur elsewhere in the home. It is worthwhile repeating the shampoo treatment, or washing the coat with lemon juice (see page 67), because the eggs, sometimes called nits, can be more resistant to treatment. An interval of two weeks between applications should be adequate to kill all lice.

You should also look carefully at the cat's diet, and try to give it a boost, using brewer's yeast and other supplements, because a heavy infestation of lice is often indicative of poor feeding.

Mange is, thankfully, not common in cats, but it can cause serious problems when it does arise, with two distinct forms being recognized. Notoedric mange, caused by a parasite known as *Notoedres cati*, causes

BELOW
A tick on a cat's ear. These are especially common in sheep-farming areas, with the cats acquiring the ticks as they move through grass.

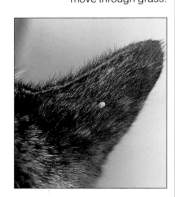

severe irritation, with the mites themselves burrowing into the skin. It is very contagious among cats. The other form of mange, called demodectic, is less likely to spread to other cats, but can prove difficult to treat successfully, whatever remedy is used. Even so, in some cases, it may resolve spontaneously.

Demodectic mange is most likely to occur on the head, with the cat pawing repeatedly at these areas. The hair becomes thinner, and if the mange is left untreated, the mites may spread down towards the body. Sulphur is often recommended as a homeopathic remedy for mange, and needs to be given for about a month. Topical treatment of the lesions with lemon juice is also to be recommended, in conjunction with the sulphur treatment.

Thallium acetas has been used to stimulate hair regrowth after mange, at a potency of 30c. It is recommended that it is given daily for a period of three weeks.

RIGHT
Some common external cat parasites. 1. Fur mite (*Cheyletiella*). 2. Harvest mite (*Trombicula*). 3. Cat louse (*Felicola*). These are uncommon in cats, although sickly kittens can be affected by them. 4. Sheep tick *(Ixodes)*.

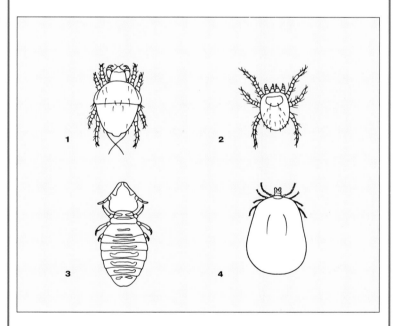

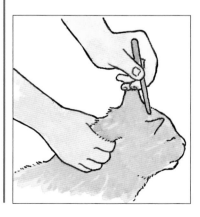

LEFT
By blocking the respiratory pore of the tick with petroleum jelly, the tick is killed, loosening its grip and falling off the cat. There is then no risk of the tick's headparts remaining *in situ*, and giving rise to a local infection. Ticks should never be pulled off while alive, except with a pair of tweezers.

INJURIES AND TRAVELLING DIFFICULTIES

Sadly, fractures among felines appear to be on the increase, many of them caused by collisions with vehicles. While it is vital to get an injured cat to the vet as quickly as possible for specialist treatment, homeopathy can help the healing process and relieve pain. Comfrey (*Symphytum officinale*) is invaluable as it helps speed up the formation of a callus at the fracture site, as well as acting as a mild analgesic.

Arnica, derived from the plant popularly known as mountain tobacco, is helpful in relieving the severe bruising which usually follows accidents. Four doses, given at hourly intervals, are recommended for initial treatment, with further tablets being used as necessary, on the following days, when the interval is increased to eight hours.

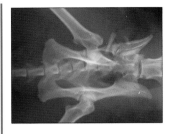

ABOVE

X-rays are valuable in determining the extent of an individual injury, and guiding a veterinarian on the best options for treatment. This cat has a fractured pelvis – a common result of a collision with a car.

LEFT

A cat which has been injured should be carried on its side, without being tipped, in case its diaphragm has been torn. Otherwise, the body organs may shift position through this gap between the chest and the abdomen. Alternatively, if the cat is restless, gently pick it up by the scruff of the neck and, supporting the rump, place it into a cardboard box or suitable carrier (**2**). If the cat struggles violently, it is a good idea to wrap it up in a towel (**3**), prior to placing it in the cat carrier.

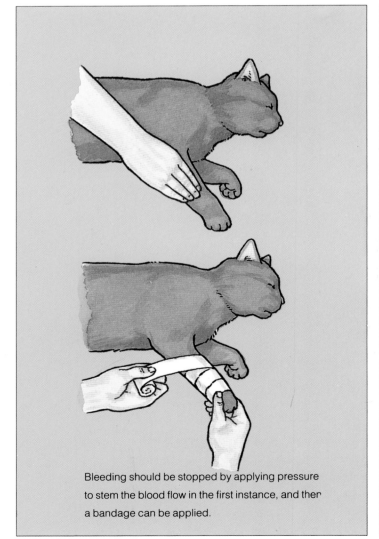

Bleeding should be stopped by applying pressure to stem the blood flow in the first instance, and then a bandage can be applied.

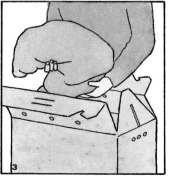

Arnica is also useful in cases of haemorrhage, although the most satisfactory way of stemming blood flow is usually to exert pressure on the area concerned, and apply calendula lotion, adding two drops to a tablespoonful of water. Where the blood flow is severe, bandaging to maintain the pressure may be helpful. *Ferrum phosphoricum* tablets can be of help, if arnica is not available, while aconite will assist in overcoming the symptoms of shock.

Similar remedies may also help heal bites inflicted in a cat fight. A bite wound should be cleaned thoroughly before using the herbal remedies.

Cats can also be quite badly hurt at home. They may burn themselves badly on a hot hob, for instance, or scald themselves, should they knock over a saucepan or kettle. There are suitable homeopathic ointments to treat burns available for emergencies, especially one made with *Urtica*, which soothes, and *Hypericum*, which has an analgesic action. Cantharis tablets are also helpful. If the injury or burn is anything other than minor, you should seek veterinary advice.

Most cats are not used to travelling and often become so distressed that they may remain difficult to handle once they arrive at their destination. Homoeopathic treatment with *Cocculus* can be helpful to prevent travel sickness, while a combination of skullcap and valerian herbs in tablet form is a herbal option to counter the problem and soothe a distressed cat. Tablets should be given before a journey, if it is known the cat will become distressed.

ABOVE

After a burn, apply cold water to the injured area, holding the affected area under a running tap if necessary. This can be critical in reducing the extent of the injury. Only then should you seek veterinary assistance.

LEFT

Cats not used to travelling, or nervous when in a car, may be given sedation before the journey (and *always* transported in a carrier!).

DIGESTIVE PROBLEMS

Cats fed on a wet diet, particularly as they get older, may suffer from a build-up of plaque on their teeth and inflamed gums, which results not only in halitosis (bad breath), but can also affect their appetite.

It may help if you can persuade your cat to allow you to brush its teeth regularly. Encouraging a routine of toothbrushing from kittenhood is most likely to be successful. Toothpastes intended for pets are pleasantly flavoured, and do not foam to the same extent as products intended for humans.

Herbal toothpaste for pets typically contains sage oil, which helps teeth to maintain their white coloration and keeps a cat's breath smelling fresh. Bad breath does not result exclusively from a problem affecting the teeth and gums, however, since it can also be linked to kidney problems.

Should the cat's gums appear badly inflamed, you should consult the vet, as it may be necessary to remove some teeth as well as clean off the tartar. The cat is likely to indicate its discomfort by eating reluctantly, and often salivating profusely.

Mercurius iodatus remedies are often favoured to reduce inflammation, with the yellow or red form being used, depending on whether the right or left side of the mouth is worse affected. A potency of 30c given three times daily for a week, is usually recommended in either case. When there are clear signs of ulceration, borax may be the correct remedy, at a potency of 6c, given twice daily over a fortnight.

ABOVE
Tartar is formed on the teeth from an accumulation of food, bacteria, and substances in the saliva. If left untreated, the roots become infected, and the teeth become loose and painful.

BOTTOM RIGHT
An inflammation of the gums is called *gingivitis* and often first shows where teeth and gums meet (**1**). It can be caused by a build-up of a hard coating of tartar on the teeth (**2**) which causes the gums to be pushed back (**3**), showing the base of the teeth and exposing pockets of space where food can collect (**4**). This is an ideal site for a secondary infection (**5**) and may lead to a more serious inflammation of the gums and a discharge (**6**). To remedy the situation, antibiotics, cleaning or even removal of the teeth and saline washes are needed.

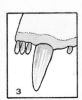

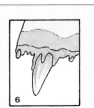

Where the cat has clear difficulty in swallowing, as distinct from chewing, an examination must be carried out to ensure this is not because of some physical obstruction at the back of the mouth. If the problem is an infection, the glands in the area are likely to be sore and swollen. *Aconitum* is often recommended for treatment at the outset, although a number of other remedies, including *Lachesis*, can be of value.

A fur ball in the stomach can also have an adverse effect on a cat's appetite, as mentioned previously. Aside from mineral oil/liquid paraffin, *Nux vomica* is sometimes used for this condition.

DIFFICULTY IN SWALLOWING

Occasional bouts of diarrhoea may occur, especially in young kittens. Withholding rich foods and offering plain foods, such as a little chicken and rice, for example, will usually overcome the problem, but if your cat's condition shows signs of deterioration, veterinary advice should be sought. Again, a range of homoeopathic remedies can be used to treat diarrhoea, with bowel nosodes often being favoured.

Constipation can either precede or follow diarrhoea, until the normal rhythm of the gut is restored. Dehydration can predispose a cat towards constipation, though it may also be a symptom of a systematic illness. A simple solution is to give olive oil on the cat's food as a laxative; homoeopathic remedies for the problem include *Bryonia*.

DIARRHOEA AND ITS AFTERMATH

URINARY TRACT PROBLEMS

ABOVE
Spraying of urine around the home and garden serves to mark a cat's territory.

One of the most widespread problems encountered with cats is their desire to spray urine indoors. This is usually a behavioural problem, rather than a medical one, being linked, in male cats, to territorial marking. Neutering may help to resolve the problem, but if this is not desired in the case of a breeding tom, then *Ustillago maydis* may be helpful. This homoeopathic remedy needs to be given three times a week, for a month, using a potency of 200c.

Spraying may continue for a period after neutering has been carried out, and Staphisagria can be useful at this stage, a dose of 7c being administered three times a day, for a week initially, although it can be continued at a higher potency less frequently for up to a month. It is

SPRAYING

also important to clean up thoroughly where the cat has been spraying so it will not be encouraged to reinforce the scent marking by spraying again in the same place.

Choose the disinfectant for the purpose carefully, because some simply reinforce the scent. White vinegar is suitable, in contrast to ammonia, which should be avoided. Bleach is also effective, depending on the surface concerned. Blot away as much of the urine as possible and wash the area several times, to remove all traces of urine. Should the condition persist, it may be necessary to resort to potentized hormones, such as folliculinum and testosterone, for a month.

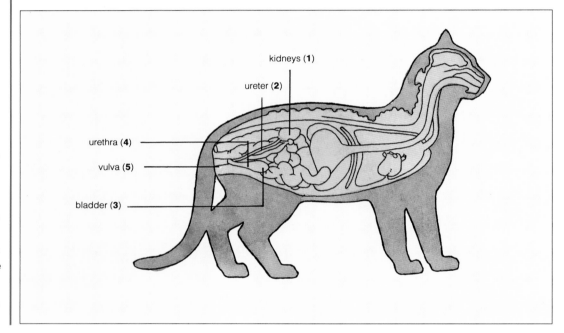

RIGHT

The urinary system in both sexes in a cat, consists of the paired kidneys (**1**), ureters (**2**), bladder (**3**) and urethra (**4**), which opens at the tip of the penis in the male whereas in the female *(above)* it opens at the vulva (**5**).

URINARY TRACT BLOCKAGE/FUS

Although it can be difficult with a cat which spends much of its time outside, you should try to check that it urinates without any apparent difficulty. A cat which attempts to urinate repeatedly, passes very little and cries out in pain is likely to be suffering from a blockage in the urinary tract. Rapid veterinary attention is essential, because the bladder could rupture, spilling urine into the abdomenal cavity.

To help a cat recover from treatment for urinary stones, called calculi, and hopefully prevent any recurrence, *Hydrangea* can be useful at a potency of 30c. It should be given daily over a period of three weeks. A number of other homeopathic remedies are also considered helpful to counter urolithiasis, as this problem is known. They include *Urtica urens* and *Calcarea phosphorica*, which may be used as a preventative in young cats.

ABOVE
A cat will crouch down with its back straight when urinating under normal circumstances.

Inflammation of the bladder, or cystitis, is another very painful condition, particularly in acute cases, and may produce similar symptoms to urolithiasis. *Aconitum* helps to overcome the pain when used at a potency of 10m. Five doses need to be given, at half hourly intervals, if there is a sign of any purulent material discolouring the urine.

INFLAMMATION OF THE BLADDER

In any problem involving the urinary tract, it is helpful to provide a urine sample for your vet, in order to estabish the most satisfactory course of treatment. This will require forward planning on your part because cats rarely cooperate, particularly if they are in pain. Have ready a shallow container, such as a small disposable plate, covered with kitchen foil. When the cat squats in its litter tray place the plate under its rear end and catch any urine.

You will also need a clean, screw-topped glass or plastic container, ideally one with a fairly narrow diameter – your vet will be able to provide you with a suitable receptacle, if necessary. By carefully creating a funnel from the foil on the plate, you can channel the urine safely into the container.

On occasions, blood may be apparent in the urine. This is likely to be linked to a problem such as acute cystitis. Diagnosis of the urine will establish the cause and the treatment required and prevent the problem becoming chronic. If this occurs, the bladder walls become thickened, and the cat will urinate more frequently than usual, passing smaller volumes. You should always be on the alert for such signs if your cat has previously suffered from cystitis, because it is a condition which can recur.

CATCHING URINE SAMPLES

While kidney function invariably deteriorates as a cat becomes older, there is also the risk of kidney infections at any age. The cat will adopt a characteristically hunched posture, be reluctant to walk, and its back will be tender when touched.

While *Aconitum* is again potentially helpful to counter this discomfort, *Apis mellifica*, given at a potency of 10m, in four doses at hourly intervals, may bring more direct relief.

Eel serum can encourage urinary output, which makes it useful in cases of acute nephritis. A potency of 30c, given three times daily over a period of three days, is usually recommended in such cases.

TREATING KIDNEY INFECTIONS

KIDNEY FAILURE IN OLDER CATS

In older cats, impairment of kidney function will be inevitable, and the typical symptoms associated with chronic nephritis will then become apparent. Weight loss may be most apparent, with the cat also suffering from halitosis (bad breath). By this stage, it is likely that at least 70 per cent of the kidney tissue is not working effectively, so that instead of being excreted from the body in urine, waste products of protein metabolism build up in the blood.

In addition, because the kidneys are no longer able to concentrate urine effectively, water is lost from the body, with the urine being dilute and of greater volume than normal. This makes the cat thirsty, and its fluid intake may well increase markedly, if it is not to suffer from dehydration. It may be sick, and appear rather dull, with its coat condition also deteriorating.

While there is no cure for kidney failure in old cats, you can help to alleviate the symptoms, by adjusting the cat's diet. You should reduce the amount of protein, so as to decrease the burden on the kidneys. Offer foods which have a higher carbohydrate content, if possible, although not all cats are keen to adapt their feeding habits. You should also supplement their vitamin intake, because water-soluble vitamins are often lost through the kidneys.

Where there is ulceration in the mouth, and as a general treatment, *Natrum muriaticum* is often recommended. This needs to be given over a relatively long period, at progressively higher potencies, starting at 200c for a month, with the treatment being administered three times a week. Then the potency should be increased to 10m, for a similar duration, and finally Cm. Even so, it is important to bear in mind that there is no curative treatment available; it may be possible to stabilize the cat's condition, perhaps for a year or two, before there is a final, terminal decline.

GLOMERULONEPHRITIS

Cats can sometimes suffer from another kidney complaint, known as glomerulonephritis, which results in swelling of the lower parts of the limbs and the abdomen. This is an immune system disease, and although it can ultimately progress to chronic renal failure, treatment in the initial stages is very different from that for kidney failure. This is because glomerulonephritis causes a loss of protein from the body via the kidneys. As a result, a high-protein diet is indicated, to prevent the cat's condition deteriorating.

CARDIOVASCULAR COMPLAINTS

Actual heart disease is not especially common in cats, with the most common condition being cardiomyopathy, which is a failure of the heart muscle to pump effectively. This can give rise to blood clots forming within the circulatory system, because of the stasis of blood in the chambers of the heart. The clot may then be passed out into the arteries, causing a blockage, called a thrombosis.

THROMBOSIS

The most common site for a thrombosis in cats is where the aorta divides to supply the hind legs, giving rise to the condition known as iliac thrombosis. The loss of blood supply causes the limb to feel cold, and there is also no pulse.

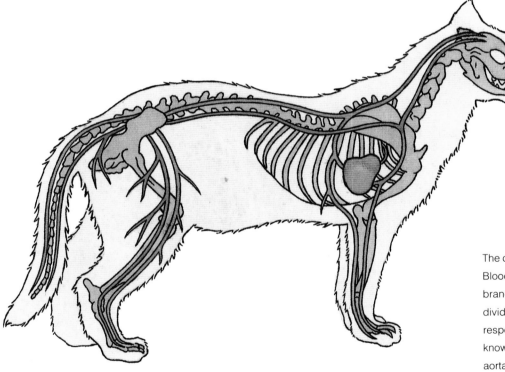

The cat's circulatory system. Blood clots in the terminal branches of the aorta, where it divides into the rear legs, are responsible for the condition known as iliac thrombosis. The aorta is part of the arterial system, shown in red, whereas the venous system is shown in blue.

Homoeopathic vets rely on a range of treatments derived from snake venom to deal with this condition and to break down the clot, and may achieve excellent results. *Crotalus horridus* is widely used, being given at a high potency of 10m, twice daily over five days. Secale is then favoured to ensure healthy blood flow continues, once the condition has been cured. A potency of 200c, given three times a week for a month, is usually advised in such cases.

Where pain and paralysis are highly evident, *Vipera* is a frequently used homeopathic remedy. A dose with a potency of 1m should be given with the same frequency as recommended for Secale. If the left leg is more severely affected, with accompanying signs of cyanosis, reflected by a bluish discoloration of the skin, then *Lachesis* may be preferred. Treatment in this case is shorter, with a 30c potency being used twice daily for 10 days.

VALVULAR PROBLEMS

Valvular problems affecting the heart are decidedly uncommon in cats, but have been known. Again, veterinary diagnosis and treatment will be required. Several homoeopathic treatments may be of value in such cases. Where the cat may be suffering from breathlessness as well as an irregular pulse, then *Lycoplus* may be given. The potency in this case is 3x, being administered twice daily for 30 days. In contrast, if the pulse is weak and rapid, *Lilium tigrinum* is favoured, using a potency of 3c. Two separate doses need to be given each day for 30 days.

ANAEMIA

A shortage of red blood cells in the circulatory system, known as anaemia, can result from a variety of causes. It may arise from blood loss as a result of injury, in which case it is called haemorrhagic anaemia. Provided that the blood flow can be stemmed, then the cat should recover uneventfully.

The use of a coagulent will help to stem the loss of blood before it becomes life-threatening. The lack of oxygen in the circulatory system, resulting from the shortage of red blood cells, causes weakness. This can also arise from warfarin poisoning, in which the poison interferes with the blood clotting mechanisms and

RIGHT

An extremely healthy appearance is no guarantee that a cat may not be suffering from anaemia: a closer look at the mouth membranes will give some indication.

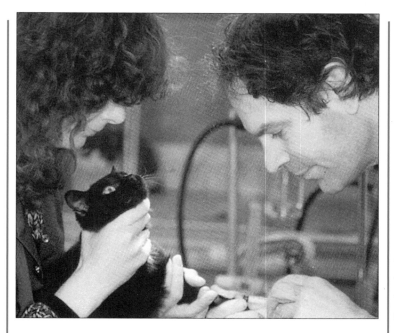

LEFT
Cats affected by anaemia have pale mucous membranes, which are whitish rather than pink. An accurate picture of the problem can be established by means of a blood test. This is a straightforward procedure, which does not usually require the cat to be sedated, although this may sometimes be necessary.

results in spontaneous haemorrhages. The lack of red blood cells in the circulation can result also in the inside of the mouth being very pale, although because the mucous membranes and gums of most cats are often pale, this need not be a sign of anaemia.

The red blood cells themselves are produced in bone marrow, and any disease affecting this tissue can result in a depressed output of red blood cells and lead to what is known as hypoplastic anaemia. This can result either from dietary deficiencies of the key ingredients needed for the manufacture of red blood cells, such as iron, or because of the toxic effects of some drugs. The effects are unlikely to be evident in the short term, because red blood cells have a life-span of just under 12 weeks.

NEVER USE ASPIRIN!

CATS CANNOT BREAK DOWN A NUMBER OF DRUGS VERY EFFECTIVELY IN THE LIVER, THEREBY DETOXIFYING THEM. THESE MAY THEN ACCUMULATE, AND EXERT A HARMFUL EFFECT ON THE BONE MARROW. ASPIRIN IS AMONG THE MOST DANGEROUS OF THESE DRUGS, AND IS TOXIC TO CATS. NOT ONLY IS IT LIKELY TO CAUSE HAEMORRHAGING, ESPECIALLY IN THE GASTROINTESTINAL TRACT, BUT IT ALSO DEPRESSES BONE MARROW ACTIVITY, TO THE EXTENT THAT RED BLOOD CELLS CANNOT BE REPLACED. ASPIRIN SHOULD THEREFORE NEVER BE GIVEN TO CATS. THE ANTIBIOTIC CHLORAMPHENICOL ALSO HAS A DEPRESSANT EFFECT ON BONE MARROW.

If a cat is suspected to be suffering from anaemia, a blood test to establish the type of anaemia is an essential first step. In some cases, the red blood cells may actually be destroyed directly in the circulation, as the result of a parasitic infection, for example, or as the result of poisoning, giving rise to the condition known as haemolytic anaemia. Treatment must then be directed to resolving the individual cause, although the use of vitamin supplements, particularly vitamin E and the B group vitamins, can be of help in all cases.

Anaemia can also be a complication associated with Feline Leukaemia Virus. This is because the virus can damage both the haemapoetic tissue in the bones, and may also destroy red blood cells directly. The prognosis in such cases is very poor.

RESPIRATORY PROBLEMS

VIRAL INFECTIONS

The most serious respiratory disorders in cats are the result of viral infections, such as Feline Viral Rhinotracheitis (FVR). All cats should receive protection against such infections, which can be serious and result in long-term complications.

It has become increasingly clear in recent years that aside from viruses, *Chlamydia* can be an important component of respiratory disease in cats. The resulting infection, known as chlamydiosis, typically affects the upper respiratory tract, causing an often severe conjunctivitis and an unpleasant rhinitis as well, with young kittens often displaying the most severe symptoms. There is a risk that this infection could also be transmissible to people, so care should be taken when dealing with a sick cat. Always wash your hands thoroughly immediately after handling it.

Bathing the eyes is important, so that the cat can continue to see without too much difficulty. *Argentum nitricum*, administered at a potency of 30c, can be of use under such circumstances. A daily dose for 10 days will be required.

BELOW
Protection against the killer viral diseases will be essential if your cat is to go into a cattery for any period of time. You will need to provide veterinary certification to this effect.

Bacterial contamination will almost inevitably result in the rhinitis becoming muco-purulent; again, bathing of the nostrils will be important in assisting the cat's recovery. *Kali bichromicum* is valuable in cases of nasal congestion, with a potency of 200c. The dose needs to be given twice a week for a month to assist recovery. Where chlamydiosis is confirmed, there is a nosode available, which needs to be given daily for 10 days. The potency normally recommended is 30c, and it can be administered alongside specific remedies.

It is not uncommon for some breeds, especially the Oriental ones, including the Siamese, which have encountered a respiratory infection early in life, to be left with chronic sinusitis. This flares up from time to time, resulting in an unpleasant discharge from the nostrils.

It can be a difficult problem to overcome, whatever method of treatment is used. When a bout does occur, *Lemna minor,* at a potency of 6c, given three times daily over five days may lead to a speedy resolution, and can stop any accompanying sneezing. Another remedy which may be advised is *Silicea,* which can help to overcome stubborn cases. A dose of 200c potency needs to be given three times a week for a month.

SINUSITIS

Other upper respiratory tract problems that may arise include pharyngitis, in which the pharyngeal region becomes swollen, usually as the result of infection, making it difficult for the cat to swallow easily. This may well be accompanied by a temperature raised above the cat's normal figure of about 38.6°C (101.5°F).

Mercurius cyanatus, at a potency of 30c, can relieve pharyngitis. The dose is given twice daily over a three-day period. If symptoms are noticeable elsewhere, affecting the eyes for example, then *Rhus toxicodendron* may be indicated. A potency of 1m will need to be given in a daily dose for two weeks. In chronic or refractory cases, a *Streptococcus* nosode can be used as well, in the form of a 30c dose administered each day for five days.

Laryngitis, resulting in the cat's losing its voice, may also occur, sometimes being so severe that the cat has difficulty in swallowing. There are several treatments that can be applied, depending on the degree of infection. *Apis mellifica* may be administered in cases where the area is badly swollen, If the cat is coughing, but not producing mucus, then *Spongia tosta* may be the preferred remedy, while in more extreme cases, *Drosera rotundifolia* might be recommended. *Calcarea fluorica* is recommended to assist the healing process, being given at a potency of 30c, three times a week for a month. Garlic tablets are also considered beneficial to assist recovery from upper respiratory tract ailments, either alone or in combination with fenugreek.

PHARYNGITIS

THE MATING RITUAL

A roused tom approaching a female from behind, as she rolls provocatively and treads with her front paws.

The tom grabs her by the scruff of the neck and, arching his back, mounts her, front legs first. The female twitches her tail aside.

The female also washes, voluptuously, and after some minutes she may well pat the male and they begin all over again.

Afterwards, the queen pulls forward, crying out, and turns on the male, who makes a hasty retreat and then washes.

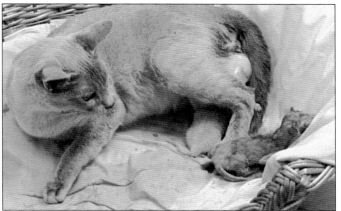

infertility, a herbal combination of damiana (*Turnera diffusa*) and Kola tablets are considered a useful tonic.

If the cat has a history of previous spontaneous abortions during pregnancy, *Viburnum opulis* will be of value in the first month. It should be a potency of 30c, given twice weekly through this stage. Subsequently, *Caulophyllum* should be given, and can also be used in the case of a difficult birth, with one dose being given every 30 minutes, for two hours.

Arnica montana is valued for helping to ensure a rapid recovery after birth, and is given at a potency of 30c, in three doses each day for two days before the birth is due. A queen's pregnancy typically lasts about 64 days, but it can vary slightly, lasting for either a slightly longer or shorter period.

Herbalists favour the use of raspberry leaf, usually in tablet form, as a means of ensuring an easy birth and assisting the queen's recovery. These are typically administered from the third week following mating until a week after the kittens are born.

If the queen appears to have difficulty in producing sufficient milk for her litter, *Urtica urens*, in the form of a 30c potency given three times daily for five days is often helpful. Other remedies which can be used on a similar basis include *Ustilago maydis* and *Agnus castus*.

Should the cause of the problem be mastitis, with the mammary glands being inflamed and swollen, then *Phytolacca decandra*, administered in 30c potency, initially three times a day for three days, and then on alternate days should help to give relief, especially if treatment begins at an early stage.

Belladonna (6c) may be indicated should the gland be badly inflamed, with five doses being given at two-hourly intervals. In long-standing cases, a better resolution may be obtained by using a 200c potency *Silicea* preparation, administered twice weekly over a six-week period.

The birth process usually proceeds uneventfully, but if there is any problem, such as a kitten being born the wrong way round, contact your vet for advice. An early call can avoid a more difficult situation arising later, should action need to be taken.

HEALTH CARE and NUTRITIONAL REFERENCE GUIDE

This section of the book summarizes the main homoeopathic treatments and the various bowel nosodes, as well as giving information about key ingredients of a cat's diet, in terms of vitamins, minerals and trace elements. In all cases of treatment, however, you should be guided by a homoeopathic veterinarian. In terms of diet, if you are using fresh foods, variety is generally the key to ensuring that your cat remains healthy and should not develop any nutritional deficiencies. Again, your veterinarian will be able to advise you if you have any particular concerns about feeding your cat, or in terms of using vitamin and mineral supplements. Overdosing with such products can be harmful.

VITAMINS, MINERALS AND TRACE ELEMENTS

The following tables summarize the key ingredients required in a cat's diet, how these can be obtained from different foods, and their functions in the body.

VITAMIN	DIETARY SOURCES FOR CATS	TYPICAL FUNCTIONS
FAT SOLUBLE GROUP	Stored in the liver with any excess likely to be harmful	—
PRE-FORMED A	BUTTER, CHEESE, EGG YOLK, LIVER, COD LIVER OIL, WHOLE MILK	Improves resistance to infection. Healthy vision. Assists protein synthesis. Important also for healthy skin, coat and respiratory system
VITAMIN D	DAIRY PRODUCTS, EGG YOLK, COD LIVER OIL	Absorption of calcium and phosphorus from the intestinal tract and metabolism in the body. Healthy bones and teeth. Growth and production of thyroid hormones.
VITAMIN E	EGG YOLK, WHEATGERM AND OTHER VARIOUS OILS SUCH AS SUNFLOWER, SAFFLOWER AND SESAME OILS, DARK GREEN VEGETABLES	Protects vital components of the body against oxidation. Helps to assist normal functioning of the reproductive system. Assists pancreatic function. Helps to prevent blood clots in the circulatory system.
VITAMIN K	WHOLE MILK, EGGS, FISH LIVER OILS, KELP, MEAT, POLYUNSATURATED OILS	Assists liver function, and the health of the body's blood clotting mechanism.
WATER-SOLUBLE GROUP	Not generally stored in the body to any significant extent.	—
B GROUP COMPRISING: B1 (THIAMINE) B2 (RIBOFLAVIN) B3 (NICOTINIC ACID) B5 (PANTOTHENIC ACID) B6 (PYRIDOXINE) B12 (CYANOCOBALAMIN) BIOTIN, INOSITOL, CHLOLINE, PABA FOLIC ACID	BREWER'S YEAST AND EXTRACTS, EGG YOLK, DAIRY PRODUCTS, WHEATGERM, FISH, OFFAL. (Supplements contain all members of the group, with brewer's yeast and extract being most valuable for this purpose)	Important in many metabolic processes in the body. Significant for healthy red blood cells.
VITAMIN C (ASCORBIC ACID)	FRUIT AND VEGETABLES INCLUDING PARSLEY, WATERCRESS AND ROSEHIPS	Helps the body's resistance to disease. Also leads to healthy teeth and bones, and of value to the circulatory system.

MINERAL/ TRACE ELEMENTS	DIETARY SOURCES FOR CATS	TYPICAL FUNCTIONS
CALCIUM	MILK, WHEATGERM, CHEESE, BREWER'S YEAST	Healthy skeletal structure and blood clotting, as well as muscular contractions.
CHROMIUM (TRACE ELEMENT)	LIVER, CHEESE, BREWER'S YEAST	Immune system. Brain and nervous functions.
COPPER (TRACE ELEMENT)	MEAT, BREWER'S YEAST, CEREALS	Blood, healthy pigmentation absorption of iron and various metabolic processes.
IODINE (TRACE ELEMENT)	KELP, GARLIC, MILK, SEAFOODS, EGGS	Production of thyroid hormones which have a key role in the body's metabolism.
IRON	BREWER'S YEAST, EGG YOLK, LIVER, LEAN MEAT, WATERCRESS	Vital for haemoglobin – the oxygen-carrying component of red blood cells, with a deficiency causing anaemia.
MAGNESIUM	FISH, SEAFOODS, WHEATGERM, BREWER'S YEAST	Helps to protect against stress. Important for synthesis of hormones, and assists healing.
MANGANESE (TRACE ELEMENT)	OFFAL, WATERCRESS, SEAWEED, WHEATGERM	Vital for the correct functioning of the brain and nervous system. Also has metabolic functions.
PHOSPHORUS	EGGS, DAIRY PRODUCTS, OFFAL, WHEATGERM, BREWER'S YEAST	Present in every living cell forming phosphotipid membranes, and occurs in association with calcium in the musculo-skeletal system. Vital for various metabolic processes as well.
POTASSIUM	KELP, GREEN, LEAFY VEGETABLES, WHEATGERM	Essential for muscle contraction and cell metabolism, also for the transmission of nerve impulses.
SELENIUM (TRACE ELEMENT)	FISH, BROWN RICE, EGGS, GARLIC, BREWER'S YEAST	Important especially for male reproductive tract, and protecting against oxidative processes which could destroy fat soluble vitamins, for example, in conjunction with Vitamin E.
SODIUM	SALT, YEAST EXTRACTS, BACON, KELP, SMOKED FISH AND MANY PROCESSED FOODS	Regulates acidity level of the blood, ensures muscle contractility and transmission of nerve impulses. Maintains body's osmotic pressure.
ZINC	BROWN RICE, HERRING, BREWER'S YEAST, EGGS, SEAFOOD AND DAIRY PRODUCTS	Correct functioning of the reproductive system. Assists the healing process, glandular activity and metabolic processes.

A–Z OF HOMOEOPATHIC REMEDIES

This table sets out a range of homoeopathic treatments, their origins and the likely ailments which they can be used to treat. Homoeopathy tends to be used more widely in veterinary medicine than herbalism, because treatments are often easier to administer, and dosing is less arduous.

SOURCE	COMPONENT	APPLICATIONS
Abies canadensis (Hemlock Spruce)	BARK AND BUDS	Digestive ailments
Abrotanum (Southernwood)	FRESH LEAVES	Joint ailments Intestinal parasites
Absinthum (Wormwood)		Epilepsy and disorders of the central nervous system
Achillea millefolium (Yarrow)	WHOLE PLANT	Haemorrhaging
Acidum salicylicum (Salicylic acid)	POWDER	Joint ailments Gastric haemorrhage
Aconitum napellus (Monkshood)	WHOLE PLANT	Shock
Actaea racemosa (Black Snake Root)	RESIN	Muscular ailments
Adonis vernalis (False Hellebore)	WHOLE PLANT	Cardiac and respiratory disorders
Aesculus hippocastanum (Horse Chestnut)	ENTIRE SEED CAPSULE	Liver ailments and cardiac disease
Agaricus muscarius (Fly Agaric)	WHOLE FUNGUS	Joint ailments Muscular cramp
Agnus castus (Chaste Tree)	RIPE BERRIES	Sexual problems
Aletris farinosa (Star Grass)	ROOT SYSTEM	Female reproductive disorders
Allium cepa (Onion)	ENTIRE PLANT	Upper respiratory tract infections
Alumen (Potash Alum)	CRYSTALS	Central nervous system disorders
Ammonium carbonicum (Ammonium carbonate)	SALT	Respiratory conditions
Ammonium causticum (Hydrate of Ammonia)	SALT	Respiratory and cardiac complaints
Angustura vera	BARK	Musculo–skeletal problems
Antimonium arsenicosum (Arsenate of Antimony)	SALT	Pneumonia and other respiratory complaints such as emphysema

SOURCE	COMPONENT	APPLICATIONS
Antimonium crudum (Sulphide of Antimony)	SALT	Skin swellings
Antimonium tartaricum (Tartar emetic)	SALT	Respiratory system ailments
Apis mellifica (Bee venom)	WHOLE INSECT OR VENOM	Swellings
Apocynum cannabinum (Indian Hemp)	WHOLE PLANT	Respiratory and cardiac problems Uro-genital system disorders
Argentum nitricum (Silver Nitrate)	SALT	Ophthalmic ailments and blood disorders
Arnica montana (Leopard's Bane)	WHOLE PLANT	Injuries, bruising and haemorrhages
Arsenicum album (Arsenic Trioxide)	SALT	Coccidiosis and skin ailments
Arsenicum iodatum (Iodide of Arsenic)	SALT	Respiratory problems refractory to other remedies
Atropinum (Belladonna alkaloid)		Opthalmic conditions
Baptisia tinctoria (Wild indiso)	BARK AND ROOT	Septicaemic conditions
Baryta carbonica (Barium carbonate)	SALT	Respiratory system ailments
Baryta muriatica (Barium chloride)	SALT	Ear infections Glandular swellings
Belladonna (Deadly Nightshade)	WHOLE PLANT WHEN IN FLOWER	Fever
Bellis perennis (Daisy)	WHOLE PLANT	Muscular ailments including sprains and bruises
Benzoicum acidum (Benzoic acid)	GUM	Urinary tract problems
Berberries vulgaris (Barberry)	ROOT BARK	Liver and kidney ailments, especially where there is jaundice
Beryllium	METAL	Viral pneumonia
Bothrops lanceolatus (Yellow viper)	VENOM	Haemorrhages of septic causation Prevention of gangrene
Bromium (Bromine)	SOLUTION	Laryngeal and mucous membrane ailments of the respiratory tract
Bryonia alba (White Bryony)	ROOTS, BEFORE FLOWERING OCCURS	Respiratory diseases
Bufo bufo (Common Toad)	SKIN VENOM	Epilepsy and hyper-sexuality

SOURCE	COMPONENT	APPLICATIONS
Cactus grandiflorus (Night-blooming Cereus)	STEMS AND FLOWERS	Cardio-vascular disease
Calcarea carbonica (Calcium carbonate)	SALT	Skeletal problems
Calcarea fluorica (Fluorspar)	SALT	Bone diseases such as actinobacillosis
Calcarea iodata (Calcium iodide)	SALT	Glandular disease
Calcarea phosphorica (Calcium phosphate)	SALT	Musculo-skeletal disorders, especially of kittens
Calc. Renalis Phosph *Calc. Renalis Uric*	SALTS	Stones in the urinary tract, often in conjunction with other remedies
Calendula officinalis (Marigold)	LEAVES AND FLOWERS	Wounds, ulcers, eye ailments
Camphora (Camphor)	GUM	Enteritis, especially caused by *Salmonella* bacteria
Cannabis sativa (American Hemp)	FLOWERING TOPS	Cardiac and urinary problems
Cantharis (Spanish Fly)	WHOLE INSECT	Kidney and bladder inflammation
Capsella bursa-pastoris (Shepherd's Purse)	WHOLE PLANT	Cystitis
Carbo vegetabilis (Vegetable charcoal)	BURNT PLANT MATERIAL	Venous circulatory disorders
Carduus marianus (St Mary's Thistle)	SEEDS	Liver ailments, especially cirrhosis
Caulophyllum (Blue Cohosh)	ROOT	Female reproductive tract problems
Causticum (Potassium Hydroxide)	SALT	Neuro-muscular system disorders
Ceanothus americanus (New Jersey Tea)	FRESH LEAVES	Splenic conditions
Chelidonium (Greater Celandine)	WHOLE PLANT AT FLOWING STAGE	Jaundice and other liver ailments
Chimaphilla umbellata (Ground Holly)	WHOLE PLANT	Uro-genital tract problems
Chininum Sulphuricum (Sulphate of Quinine)	SALT	Ear and other recurrent infections
Chionanthus virginica (Fringe Tree)	SALT	Liver ailments cirrhosis
Cinchona officinalis (Peruvian Bark)	BARK	Debility and fluid loss

SOURCE	COMPONENT	APPLICATIONS
Cinnabaris (Mercuric Sulphide)	SALT	Ophthalmic conditions Superficial uro-genital complaints
Cicuta virosa (Water Hemlock)	ROOT DURING FLOWERING PERIOD	Nervous diseases
Cineraria maritima (Dusty Miller)	WHOLE PLANT	Ophthalmic conditions
Cocculus (Indian Cockle)	SEEDS	Travel sickness
Coccus cacti (Cochineal)	BODIES OF FEMALE INSECTS	Respiratory and urinary tract ailments
Colchicum autumnale (Meadow Saffron)	BULB	Allergies and anti-inflammatory treatment
Colocynthis (Bitter Cucumber)	FRUIT	Digestive disturbances, especially diarrhoea
Condurango (Condor Plant)	BARK	Internal malignancies
Cornium maculatum (Hemlock)	WHOLE PLANT	Paralysis
Convallaria majoris (Lily of the Valley)	WHOLE PLANT	Valvular heart disease
Copaiva (Balsam of Peru)	BALSAM	Pyelonephritis, cystitis and urethritis
Crataegus (Hawthorn)	RIPE FRUIT	Arrhythmic heart conditions
Crotalus horridus (Rattlesnake)	VENOM	Septicaemia and snake-bite
Croton tiglium	SEEDS	Disgestive disturbances especially diarrhoea
Cubeba officinalis (Cubebs)	UNRIPE FRUIT	Uro-genital problems
Cuprum aceticium (Copper acetate)	SALT	Muscle weakness
Cuprum metallicium (Copper)	METAL	Central nervous system disorders especially epilepsy
Curare (Arrow poison)	FROG'S SKIN	Muscular paralysis
Datura stramonium (Thorn Apple)	WHOLE FRESH PLANT AND ITS FRUIT	Central nervous system disorders, where sense of balance is affected
Digitalis purpurea (Foxglove)	LEAVES	Cardiac failure resulting from valvular disorders
Drosera rotundifolia (Sundew)	WHOLE PLANT	Lymphatic conditions Inflammation of the larynx

SOURCE	COMPONENT	APPLICATIONS
Echinacea angustifolia (Rudbeckia)	WHOLE PLANT	Septicaemia and toxaemia
Eel serum	SERUM	Toxaemia and kidney disorders
Epigea repens (Trailing arbutus)	FRESH LEAVES	Urethral and bladder stones
Euphrasia officinalis (Eyebright)	WHOLE PLANT	Conjunctivitis, corneal ulceration
Ferrum iodatum (Iodide of iron)	SALT	Iron deficiency
Ferrum phosphoricum (Ferric phosphate)	SALT	Febrile illnesses; pulmonary congestion
Ficus religiosa (Rubber Plant)	LEAVES	Haemorrhages. Also sometimes coccidiosis
Fluoricum acidum (Hydrofluoric acid)	SALT	Ulcers; necrotic bone disease
Formica (Formic acid)	LIVE ANTS	Joint ailments
Gelsemium sempervirens (Yellow Jasmine)	ROOT BARK	Muscle tremors and resulting weakness
Glonoinum (Nitroglycerine)	CHEMICAL	Heat stroke
Graphites (Black Lead)	CHEMICAL	Eczema
Hamamelis virginica (Witch Hazel)	FRESH BARK OF TWIGS AND ROOTS	Bruising; venous system disorders
Hecla Lava (Hecla)	VOLCANIC ASH	Bone tumours; dental disease
Helleborus niger (Christmas Rose)	ROOT JUICE	Cardiac rhythm disorders
Hepar Sulphuris Calcareum (Impure Calcium Sulphide)	CALCIUM CARBONATE BURNT WITH FLOWERS OF SULPHUR	Purulent conditions
Hydrangea arborescens (Hydrangea)	FRESH YOUNG SHOOTS AND LEAVES	Urolithasis
Hydrastis canadensis (Golden Seal)	ROOT	Catarrhal and other mucopurulent discharges
Hydrocotyle asiatica (Indian Pennywort)	WHOLE PLANT	Skin ailments Female genital disorders
Hyoscyamus niger (Henbane)	WHOLE PLANT	Hyperexcitability
Hypericum perforatum (St John's Wort)	WHOLE PLANT	Nerve damage linked to lacerated wounds. Spinal injury in the coccygeal area

SOURCE	COMPONENT	APPLICATIONS
Iodium (Iodine)	TINCTURE	Ovarian problems. Glandular treatments, especially for the thyroid
Ipecacuanha	DRIED ROOT	Haemorrhages and use post-partum
Iris versicolor (Blue Flag)	FRESH ROOT	Glandular disorders, especially those affecting the pancreas
Kali arsenicum (Potassium arsenite)	SALT	Eczema and other skin conditions
Kali bichromicum (Potassium dichromate)	SALT	Sinusitis, broncho-pneumonia and pyelonephritis
Kali carbonicum (Potassium carbonate)	SALT	Weakness
Kali chloricum (Potassium chlorate)	SALT	Urinary tract problems
Kali hydriodicum (Potassium iodide)	SALT	Ophthalmic and respiratory disorders
Kreosotum (Beechwood Creosote)	SOLUTION	Ulceration and likely gangrenous states
Lachesis (Bushmaster)	VENOM	Haemorrhage and sepsis
Lathyrus sativus (Chick Pea)	FLOWER AND SEED PODS	Local paralysis and possible mineral deficiencies
Ledum palustre (Marsh Tea)	WHOLE PLANT	Eye injuries and puncture wounds
Lemna minor (Duckweed)	WHOLE PLANT	Catarrhal complications and flatulence
Lilium tigrinum (Tiger Lily)	LEAVES AND FLOWERS	Pyometra
Lithium carbonicum (Lithium carbonate)	SALT	Arthritis and some urinary ailments
Lobelia inflata (Indian Tobacco)	DRIED LEAVES	Emphysema and as a recovery stimulant
Lycoplus virginicus (Bugle Weed)	WHOLE PLANT	Cardiac problems and raised blood pressure
Lycopodium clavatum (Club Moss)	SPORES	Pneumonia, alopecia and loss of appetite resulting from liver problems
Magnesia phosphorica (Phosphate of magnesium)	SALT	Muscular spasms
Melilotus (Sweet Clover)	WHOLE PLANT	Haemorrhaging
Mercurius (Mercurius solubilis)	METAL	Anaemia and diarrhoea

SOURCE	COMPONENT	APPLICATIONS
Mercurius corrosivus (Mercuric chloride)	SALT	More potent than mercurius; possibly useful for coccidiosis
Mercurius cyanatus (Cyanate of mercury)	SALT	Toxic conditions, arising from bacterial infections
Mercurius dulcis (Calomel)	SALT	Ear and liver ailments; including mild cirrhosis
Mercurius iodatus flavus (Yellow Iodide of mercury)	SALT	Salivary gland swellings and similar glandular disorders
Mercurius iodatus ruber (Red Iodide of mercury)	SALT	Muscular stiffness in the neck and glandular swellings
Murex purpurea (Cuttlefish)	INK SAC	Regulates female reproductive cycle and counters cystic ovaries
Muriatic acid (Hydrochloric acid)	SOLUTION	Septicaemia and ulceration
Naja tripudians (Cobra)	VENOM	Cardiac problems resulting in oedema
Natrum muriaticum (Sodium chloride)	SALT	Chronic nephritis and anaemia
Natrum sulphoricum (Nitric acid)	SALT	Liver ailments; head injuries
Nux vomica (Poison Nut)	SEEDS	Digestive problems
Ocimum canum	LEAVES	Urinary complaints
Opium (Poppy)	POWDER	Nervous system disorders
Palladium	METAL	Female reproductive system especially for inflamed ovaries
Pancreas	GLANDULAR EXTRACT	Pancreatic disorders
Pareira (Velvet Leaf)	FRESH ROOT	Bladder stones
Petroleum (Rock Spirit)	OIL	Dry skin and eczema
Phosphoricum acidum (Phosphoric acid)	SOLUTION	Combats diarrhoea and flatulence
Phosphorus	ELEMENT	Wide-ranging
Phytolacca decandra (Pore Root)	WHOLE PLANT	Glandular swellings, especially mastitis
Platina (Platinum)	METAL	Female genital tract; inflamed ovaries
Plumbum metallicum (Lead)	METAL	Renal deterioration with hepatic involvement. Central nervous system disorders

SOURCE	COMPONENT	APPLICATIONS
Podophyllum peltatum (May Apple)	Whole plant	Gastro-intestinal conditions affecting kittens
Ptelea (Water Ash)	Root or bark	Stomach and liver ailments
Pulsatilla (Anemone)	Whole flowering plant	Catarrh and some female reproductive disorders
Ranunculus bulbosus (Buttercup)	Whole plant	Muscular ailments and skin conditions
Rhododendron (Snow Rose)	Fresh leaves	Stiffness and orchitis
Rhus toxicodendron (Poison Oak)	Fresh leaves	Muscle and joint ailments and some skin conditions
Rumex crispus (Yellow Dock)	Fresh root	Respiratory and digestive ailments, reducing the discharge from mucous membranes
Ruta Graveolens (Rue)	Whole fresh plant	May facilitate labour, also used to assist rectal prolapses
Sabina (Savine)	Oil	Uterine conditions
Sanguinaria (Blood Root)	Fresh root	Circulatory congestive conditions and female reproductive tract disorders
Secale cornutum (Ergot of Rye)	Fresh fungus	Smooth muscle conditions affecting the uterus, including post-partum haemorrhage
Sepia officinalis (Cuttlefish)	Dried liquid from ink sac	Ringworm Encouraging maternal instincts
Silicea (Pure flint)	Element	Bone disorders
Sodium biborate (Borax)	Salt	Stomatitis and gastro-intestinal tract irritations
Solanum dulcamara (Woody Nightshade)	Fresh stems and leaves before flowering	Ringworm and kidney ailments
Solidago virga (Golden Rod)	Whole fresh plant	Renal problems
Spigelia (Pink Root)	Dried herb	Ophthalmic conditions
Spongia tosta (Roasted sponge)	Whole animal	Disorders of lymphatic system and cardiac treatment
Squilla maritima (Sea onion)	Dried bulb	Heart and kidney ailments with signs of dropsy
Staphis agria	Seeds	Hormonal eczema; cystitis
Strophanthus (Onage)	Seeds	Diuretic; improves heart action

SOURCE	COMPONENT	APPLICATIONS
Strychninum	SOLUTION	Disorders affecting the central nervous system
Sulfonal (Coal tar derivative)	SOLUTION	Central nervous system conditions affecting the state of balance
Sulphur	ELEMENT	Skin conditions including eczema and mange
Symphytum officinale (Comfrey)	WHOLE PLANT	Fractures and for ophthalmic conditions
Syzygium (Jumbul)	SEEDS	Pancreatic disorders, especially diabetes mellitus
Tabacum (Tobacco)	PLANT	Travel sickness
Tarantula hispanica (Spanish spider)	WHOLE ARTHROPOD	Excitement and excessive libido in tom cats
Tellurium	METAL	Conjunctivitis and ear ailments
Terebinthinae (Oil of Turpentine)	SOLUTION	Haemorrhaging and nephritis
Thallium acetas	SALT	Alopecia and other skin conditions
Thuja occidentalis (Arbor vitae)	FRESH TWIGS	Warty growths and related skin conditions
Turnera diffusa (Damiana)		Encourages libido
Uranium nitricum (Uranium nitrate)	SOLUTION	Pancreatitis; often in combination with *Iris versicolor*
Urtica urens (Stinging nettle)	FRESH PLANT	Urinary tract problems
Ustillago maydis (Corn Smut)	FUNGI	Uterine conditions; alopecia
Uva ursi (Bearberry)	DRIED LEAVES AND FRUIT	Disorders of the urinary tract, notably cystitis and pyelonephritis
Veratrum album (White Hellebore)	ROOTS	Cases of collapse
Viburnum opulis (Water Elder)	FRESH BARK	Smooth muscle problems; for countering repeated spontaneous abortions
Vipera (Common Viper)	VENOM	Oedema with venous congestion, making it useful in some liver conditions as well
Zincum metallicum (Zinc)	METAL	Fever and anaemia

BOWEL NOSODES

Nosodes as a group can be used both to prevent and also to treat diseases. These particular nosodes tend to be used in long-standing cases of illness, affecting particular body systems, where several other remedies could be indicated, because of the range of symptoms. High potencies are less favoured in the case of bowel nosodes than with many homoeopathic remedies. Furthermore, after a course of treatment, an interval of several months is usually indicated before the nosode is given again.

NOSODE	INDICATION	ASSOCIATED REMEDIES
Gaertner-Bach	Emaciation and malnutrition	Phosphorus; Silicea; Mercurius
Proteus-Bach	Central and peripheral nervous system	Natrium muriaticum; Cuprum metallicum
Morgan-Bach	Digestive and respiratory systems, plus skin ailments, eg eczema	Graphites; Petroleum; Psorinium; Sulphur
Dys Co-Bach	Digestive and cardiac systems	Argentum nitricum; Arsenicum album
Sycotic Co-Paterson	Ulcers on mucous membranes and skin	Mercurius corrosivus; Natrum sulphorium; Nitricum acidum; Hydrastis canadensis

INDEX